An Awesome Life of an Ordinary Man

Man

A Life Sprinkled with Miracles

by

John L. Cartier

An Awesome Life of an Ordinary Man

A Life Sprinkled with Miracles

by

John L. Cartier

PEAR
TREE
PUBLISHING

An Awesome Life of an Ordinary Man

A Life Sprinkled with Miracles

By John L. Cartier

Copyright © 2017 by John L. Cartier

Published by Pear Tree Publishing

Bradford, Massachusetts

www.PearTreePublishing.net

First Edition

Proudly published in the United States of America

Cartier, John L.
    Name / by John L. Cartier – 1st Ed.

ISBN 978-1-62502-019-2
Library of Congress Control Number: 2017936615

1. Cartier, John L. 2. Cartier, John L. – Family. 3. Cartier, John L. – Biography. 4. Massachusetts – Untied States – Biography I. Title II. Cartier, John L. – Biography

Cover & Book Design by John L. Cartier, Marie Fay and Christopher P. Obert
Photos by John L. Cartier, the Cartier family and friends.

In Memory of

Bob and Alma Amirault

&

John and Beatrice Cartier

Dedication

My wife, Laura
Our Children
Our Grandchildren
Our Great Grandchildren

Table of Contents

Chapter 1

It is April 8, 2016. I am 84 years old and I have just completed a new experience in my life, having had 33 radiation treatments for cancer of the larynx. My surgeon in Boston told me I had a 90% chance of a total recovery. The 15 minute radiation treatments involved being bolted to a board under a full helmet that covered my head and shoulders. The preparation took longer than the actual treatment. There were 6 weeks of daily treatments which gave me a considerable amount of time to reflect on my life over the past 84 years, and oh boy, what a revelation that has been for me. So, let me start from the beginning.

Birth

It was a cold, wintry day on January 16, 1932. At 2:05 AM I entered into this world weighing in at 10lbs 14ozs. Born on the second floor of a three tenement house on Victor St. in

Haverhill, MA, I was my parent's third child, having two older sisters, Jeanne, age four and Claire, age two.

The five of us existed during the fallout of the Big Depression of 1929. We were very thankful that Dad had a job as a meat cutter in a local grocery store and my mother did odd jobs sewing and house cleaning for upper class families.

Curious look even at eight months.

When I was six months old we moved to the first floor of a two tenement house on Lafayette St. My parents paid $5 a week for rent. The neighborhood had 12 two tenements with about 35 kids of all ages living there with both parents. We weren't rich but we never thought we were poor. We had a roof over our heads and food on the table. Some families were on welfare but we all shared what we had. The doors were never locked! Kids would knock and walk right in, we were all like a great big family. We were fortunate to have the WPA (Works Progress Administration) where able bodied men, who were unemployed, went to work to build sidewalks, roads and other federal projects. The CCC (Civilian Conservation Corps) was for young adults to work in the forestry sector. There was very little welfare at this time and it only went to those who could not work to support their families.

Only one telephone

Our immediate neighborhood had only one telephone which belonged to a family with a lot of kids. I remember the mother as being a large woman and her husband, a taxi driver, was very small. The mother would open her second floor window and yell to me, "Johnny, telephone!" I would run next door, up one flight of stairs and into the dining room to take my call. We didn't have a phone for several years and we didn't have a car until I was seventeen. We did, however, have a fine bus system back then to compensate!

Many streets weren't paved so the city provided tank trucks to spray the roads to hold down the dust. Horse drawn vegetable wagons, rag wagons and the ice truck were seen regularly in our neighborhood. Neighborhood kids would rush to the back of the ice truck when a delivery was being made and grab scraps of ice to chew on. My mother would place the ice card in our front window and, depending on which side faced up, the ice man determined what size ice block he delivered to us. The ice man wore a large leather apron on his back. He would back up to the ice block, grab the ice with a pair of ice grippers, and carry the ice block, on his back, into our house. My job was to keep the ice tray empty so it wouldn't overflow with water. It was quite a trick to carry and balance the full tray from the ice box to the sink without spilling.

As kids we were constantly playing outside. I still have fond memories of stick ball, tag and hide and go seek. My favorite pastime was looking for snakes in Cashman's field beyond the sand banks. I was especially fond of a green snake I found, which I brought to school with me. It happened to wiggle out of my pocket and maneuvered down the classroom aisle, causing the girls to jump in horror. No one knew it was me, until now!

I want to be an altar boy

I was born Catholic. I am a practicing Catholic and will be until I die. I have many friends of all denominations and some without any faith and I love them all. So I'm not writing this book to convert the reader, but hopefully to show you how my faith has been such an integral part of my life.

My first personal encounter with the church was when I was four years old. I desperately wanted to be an altar boy. My mother would always say to me, "Johnny, you're much too young." Well, I finally wore her down. We walked over to St Joseph's Church and met the pastor half way down the right aisle. It was about 3:00 PM and the sun was shining in! That's how vivid the encounter was for me. In spite of the fact I was only four, my mother addressed the priest, "Johnny has something to ask you." The priest answered, "Yes, Johnny, what might that be?" I answered, "I want to be an altar boy!" The priest answered, "That would be wonderful, Johnny! I will see that you become one when you are seven years old." Upset, I replied, "But Father, I want to be one now." The priest replied, "I'm sorry Johnny. The church has certain rules which we must follow. Do you understand, Johnny?" I said, "No, I don't, Father. And if you don't let me be an altar boy now, then I'll never be one." I turned around crying and ran out of the church. Did I ever become an altar boy? I'll fill you in with a later chapter.

To the beach with Lefty

Another fond memory I have is of the Verrette family that lived in our neighborhood on Thorndike St. They had a son named Lefty, a really nice guy. He had this nifty coupe with a rumble seat that opened in the back. Occasionally, with our parent's permission, Lefty would pack about five kids in his coupe and off we would go to the beach for the day. You know something, I never thought that I was assertive, but apparently I was because I always made sure that I was in the rumble seat for the trip. Open air ride, free as a bird, no seat belts, no problems, just a great time at the beach with Lefty, all expenses paid, on a beautiful summer's day. What fun! As I look back, we didn't have much, but we had a lot of fantastic memories of our early days.

Down Lafayette St., toward Hilldale Ave., stood my Dad's homestead, a stately two tenement with a repair garage on the property where my Pepere (my Dad's father) ran a motorcycle and car repair and sales business. It was also a hangout for Pepere's friends. Now you probably won't believe this but I saw it with my own eyes. Pepere's buddies would turn the car on its side so he could work under the motor, then they'd turn the car back on its wheels. The metal body was so strong it didn't damage the car. If you wanted to buy a used car, no problem, the price was $25. All models and ages were the same price, $25. He also rented out motorcycles. It was a great place to hang out to learn auto repair. I do remember an incident when, as a joke, one of Pepere's buddies picked me up with his hands from both sides of my head. I swear I've never been the same since. Those were the good old days.

As I leave my formative years and enter into my know-it-all years, my lifelong ambition was to become a mechanical engineer. It started when I was around five when I became extremely curious about what made things work. I would take apart anything I could get my hands on to see how it was made, such as a flashlight or a clock. I would try to put it back together using all the parts, which was practically impossible except for the flashlight. You will never guess what my profession turned out to be, so don't cheat and look ahead, let it be a surprise, I know it was for me.

Sledding incident

In the winter, Haverhill would block off Thorndike and Lafayette St for sledding. When I was around seven years old, a gang of us boys were sledding down Lafayette St. Unfortunately, my chin collided with the blade of the boy's sled in front of me resulting in a two inch long cut. It's strange how the area of the cut got numb and didn't hurt like you would expect. I went home and told my mother what had happened. We walked all the way to Emerson St to Dr. Simard's office to get stitched up, then we walked back home. As an adult, I told my kids, my grandchildren and now my great grandchildren that a bullet grazed my chin in the war. It makes a better story!

Flowers need care!

Our two story tenement was the last house on our street. Beyond us was a sand bank and beyond that was a huge 15 acre field. There was a hill at the far end of the field with a house sitting on it called Cashman's mansion. At the foot of the hill, next to a brook, was a large shed which housed two wagons. This was our great playground! Both the large house and the wagon shed were in perfect shape and remained that way for many years.

One day, as a few of us guys were playing in Cashman's mansion, a police cruiser came up the driveway, stopped at the house, and rounded up all the guys except for me. I was in the attic looking out the window. Two cops read my friends the riot act and told them to stay out of the house or the next time they would be taken to the station and booked for trespassing. As things settled down and the coast was clear, I calmly walked out of the house and ran home. Another time, over the summer, we set the field near Cashman's mansion on fire. When the fire department arrived, we helped put the fire out.

On the north side of Lafayette St., and just beyond our back yards, was a six foot metal fence with barbed wire on the top. Within the fence were a couple of chestnut trees and two very large gas tanks which stood about sixty feet tall. We learned to scale the fence with ease to get some chestnuts and would constantly be chased out by the tank workers, but they never caught us. We weren't destructive, just a little mischievous. It's what boys did back then.

I did, however, have to confess to our priest another certain incident involving the Cashman mansion. I wanted to please my mother so I took my wagon and went to the Cashman's abandoned house and dug up all the flowers from the front of the house. I didn't think it was stealing, just putting the flowers in a better place where they would be cared for and enjoyed. The priest kind of went along with me.

Chapter 2

How was your day dear?

Being the youngest and only boy with two sisters, you would think that I would be spoiled. My sisters, Jeanne and Claire, certainly thought so. My dad was very gentle and soft spoken compared to my mother who ran the household without exception. I suppose you would call my mother "controlling" and there can be only one of those in the household. Mom was very fun loving but she also had a serious job to do and she did it with all the power from within her. However, to this day, I can never remember them having an argument. Every day, my mother would pretty up and meet my dad at the door when he came home from work. They would kiss and hug, and my mother would always say, "How did your day go today dear?" These are the little things you never forget.

Child labor

My sisters, Jeanne and Claire, had two very different personalities. Jeanne was a prankster, loved life and was always ready for a challenge. Claire, who was born with asthma and took advantage of her ill health, was very serious and couldn't take a joke. If I did something she didn't like, which was often, she would kick me in the shins. You would think I would have caught on after a while, but I kept on annoying her and she kept on kicking me. We truly loved and respected one another and as adults learned to accept our differences. I have far more happy memories of my past than bad ones.

As I look back, I think I got the raw end of the deal. Maybe my mother was simply preparing me for the future, so I will look at it that way. My chores were as follows: polish all the copper pipes in the pantry, wash the kitchen, pantry and bathroom floors on my hands and knees every week, take out the trash, bring in the barrels, mow the lawn, and shovel the snow when needed. One good thing about not having a car, I didn't have to wash it. As for my sisters, they made their bed, washed dishes, cleaned the house and washed their hair.

Grey Nuns & mean brothers

Our grammar school had Grey Nuns teaching both girls and boys for grades 1-4. In the fifth grade the boys were separated and were taught (more like disciplined) by the Brothers. I don't know what order they belonged to but we wished they would go back to where they came from. A vivid memory involved Brother Silver, my fifth grade teacher. Brother Silver saw a boy fooling around in the back row of his class. Brother Silver took his clicker and tossed it to the back of the room. The clicker bounced off the empty desk in front of the kid and hit him smack in the middle of his forehead. We behaved and I must admit, we were very well prepared academically for high school!

Paper route with Sheba

Now that I was nine years old and ready to earn my own money, I bought a morning paper route delivering the Boston Post, the Globe and the Record. The papers were dropped off next to Comeau's Funeral Parlor at the top of Thorndike St. where I would pick them up at 6:00 AM, 7 days a week. The route was up Belleview Ave. to Blasdell St., to Broad St., to Bedford St., to Broadway, to Victor St., to Duprie Ave., back to Thorndike and home. It took around 30 to 45 minutes to complete the route. On one of my first stops, Sheba, a full grown collie, would be waiting for me and she kept me company until the end of my route. We would play together for about 5 to 10 minutes until I'd say, "Home, Sheba!", point to St. Joseph Church and off she would go. We had a love affair that lasted over 6 years until I sold the route when I was fifteen.

The big war started, so I felt that I had to do my share to support the war effort. On collection day, I asked all my customers if they would save their prior week's papers. I collected them with my cart, which had sides on it, so I could hold quite a load. My customers also agreed to save all their old rags, metal, and cooking fat, which I brought to Mohegan Market on Merrimack St. The fat was used to make bombs. Everything I collected went to the war effort except the newspapers. My father would borrow my Uncle Ray's truck about every six weeks. We would load up the truck with the old newspapers and haul them to the Haverhill Paper Mill in Bradford. The going rate was $38 a ton, in cash! On the way home my Dad would stop on Winter St. at a small watering hole for a quick beer. I would give him $2 to wet his whistle and told him to keep the change. As he departed from the truck he would look at me with a big smile and return to the truck with the same big smile.

I considered myself financially independent at nine years old. On Saturday afternoons I would go to the Lafayette theatre on Essex St. and pay 12 cents for a double feature, a news reel and a cartoon. Back then it didn't take much to be financially independent!

Plum Island voyage

My mother's very best and oldest friend was Ann Demarais, whose husband was Heck, of Heck & Joe's Diner on White St. My mother worked for them cleaning both the diner and their apartment above the diner. Several times they would call my mother and tell her to be ready in an hour – the Cartiers are going to Plum Island Basin – for a vacation free of charge! My mother would frantically run around gathering up all the essentials for a two week stay at the beach. I was about nine at the time when me and the boy next door (I instigated it) took a small rowboat for a spin. We jumped in the boat, rowed out beyond the basin, out the Merrimack River beyond the jetty and out to sea. We were picked up and towed back to the basin where the water currents were calm. The other boat owner scolded us to never do that again and we never did! We both got back to land unharmed and none the worse, so we decided not to tell our parents of the event.

Lawns, dogs, kids, oh my!

Now that I was ten years old, it was time to broaden my horizons. I wanted to contribute to the house and put a little more money in my savings account. This was a habit that I have carried throughout my life and it has proven a good one.

I started a lawn mowing service, a dog walking service and a baby sitting service, all of which I was able to accomplish while attending school. My first dog walking service was for a father and daughter who lived in a back apartment in Comeau's Funeral Home. The daughter asked me if I would walk their Boston Terrier every day since they both worked. They provided me with a key to their apartment and I walked their dog for $1 a week.

The babysitting job was for the Hennessey's on the first floor of a three tenement on Broadway. I babysat their little baby, Nancy, on most Friday or Saturday nights. I made about $1 for 5-6 hours.

Lastly, my lawn mowing job was at a much higher rate of $.50 per hour using a push mower. There weren't any fancy powered mowers back then! Putting all the jobs together, I was making about $4 per week, I was rich! Movies were $.12, bread was $.10 a loaf, and gasoline was $.15 per gallon. I was financially independent for a kid!

I bought a beautiful portable Zenith radio which, for me, cost a bundle. My sisters would borrow it to go to the beach with their friends. My sister Jeanne even bought me a great dress shirt for my birthday so SHE could wear it over her bathing suit on trips to the beach with MY radio! Aren't sisters wonderful!

Chapter 3

To the prom

I was in for a culture shock when I entered St. James High School. The student body was Italian! Irish! and Polish! just to name a few. Everyone wasn't French! I lived such a sheltered existence that it didn't dawn on me that there were other nationalities walking the face of the earth. I quickly adapted to my new environment. I joined the football team as an end, probably because I was tall. I wasn't a very good player but I did enjoy playing and being on a team.

I also decided to take exhibition ballroom dancing. My two sisters were delighted! They took me to the Teen Haven dance hall, a converted church located on Main St. just above the Paramount Theater. This was the beginning of my social life as a very young teenager. I must add that I was the only freshman at St. James, to my knowledge at the time, to ever be invited to the senior prom. Norma was the name of my

28

date. Being without wheels, I ordered a taxi to and from the prom. At least we didn't have to walk the distance with the girl's gowns and all. We had a ball dancing the whole night away! I took Norma right home after the prom, kissed her good night, she thanked me, and I never saw her again - she was from Haverhill High. Why did Norma ask me to take her to the prom? Norma and her girlfriend would go sliding on the same streets I did, so we knew each other, and she knew I was a good dancer and I was tall. I must say, I always did like older women.

Anyone for chocolate?

I started hunting for a real job in Washington Square, hitting every store requesting employment. My very first job was at the Clear-Weave woman's store on upper Merrimack St. where I worked for about one year. As I look back now, I was always very busy doing something. My next job was at Simard Pharmacy in Lafayette Square as a soda jerk and part-time sales clerk. The soda fountain had a row of stools and a couple of booths. This job I would rather forget but it's part of my earlier experiences. One of my customers at the counter ordered a chocolate frappe. I put all the necessary ingredients, including two scoops of chocolate ice cream, into the mixer. When I took the container off the mixer there was still a fair amount of ice cream left on the beater which hadn't quite stopped. Everyone in the whole store was sprayed with liquid chocolate. The initial looks on the patrons' faces said "kill the soda jerk" but then the mood turned to surprise, followed by laughter. I got both wet and dry towels to hand out to everyone to clean up the chocolate frappe. It took months before the incident was generally forgotten but I learned a big lesson, be patient and remove the frappe slowly.

Next job was with American Grocery on Essex St. They hired me as an assistant bookkeeper, warehouse worker, and truck driver. I got quite an education there. The business was run by the Giero Brothers who maintained the Italian way of life to the fullest, yelling at you one minute and loving you the next. Life was always exciting with the Giero brothers. I have many fond memories and experiences there.

American Grocery was followed by a position at Gerro's men store in Washington Square. I doubled as a stock boy and sales clerk. I was now making 75 cents an hour until Mr. Gerro asked me to work overtime and help the window dresser, who periodically would change the window display. I agreed to do it but only if I got a raise. My hourly rate increased to 80 cents. I remained there until I entered the Navy.

He's still waiting!

A funny thing happened at St. James High School when I was a sophomore. I was leaving my business class when I noticed this pretty, tall girl. I turned to my friend Bob, walking behind me, and said, "Bob, see that tall girl over there? I'm going to marry her someday." I knew nothing about her and didn't even know her name. Bob's remark was, "You know, John, I wouldn't mind taking her out myself." So we flipped a coin and I won. After getting her name, I called Laura, told her who I was and she said she knew who I was. Hmmm... very interesting. She said that she noticed me in the hallway as well. It was love at first sight for me but not for her. Laura was one of the most popular girls in school. She actually agreed to go to a movie with me. Two weeks later she got a call from one of her boyfriends for a date and told him that at present she was going out with John Cartier. The boyfriend told Laura, "I'll call you back in a couple of weeks; that will never last." He's still waiting.

Shall we dance?

I was 15 and Laura was 16 and we started going steady. My family didn't have a car, so I would walk to her house in Bradford, or she would pick me up with her family car. This was not a perfect arrangement but it worked for us. We dated every Friday night, going to movies, bowling, and hayrides. We often double dated with Jim & Rita. Lucky for us Jim had a car. Jim and I had been best friends since the fourth grade in grammar school.

The four of us started going to dance halls within a thirty mile radius. We frequented the Commodore in Lowell, the Casino in Hampton Beach, the dance hall in Canobe Lake Park, the Totem Pole in Newton, and the Rockingham Ballroom. Our favorite one, the Crystal Ballroom in North Andover, had a marble floor and a large crystal ball that rotated and made the whole room sparkle. Our signature dances were the waltz and fox trot but we did them all. After the dance we would stop at the Cozy Corner in Methuen for a hamburger and a Coke. We took trips to the beach and the White Mountains. We had loads of fun together.

Anchors Aweigh!

It was now the spring of 1950 and both Jim and I were approaching draft age due to the Korean War. Since neither of us wanted the army, we decided that when one of us got our draft notice we would both join the navy together. I got the notice first to report! Immediately I went to Harvey Wood Heel Co., which Jim's father owned on Phoenix Row, climbed up one flight of stairs and found Jim at a work bench. Jim dropped everything and the two of us marched over to the post office and joined the navy. We had never mentioned our plan to our parents so we figured it was about time we did. Their reactions weren't quite what we thought they would be. After all, we thought it was safer than the army! Our parents weren't thinking about it quite that way.

I got my appendix removed two weeks before Jim and I were called to report to Boston for our physicals. Seeing the large red scar, the doctor asked, "When did this take place, son?" I explained and eventually passed my physical. As Jim and I were waiting for our next exam, over the loud speaker came the announcement that there were two positions open in naval aviation. Those who were interested should report to room # 8. Jim and I looked at each other and decided, why not? We applied and got the assignments. After basic training in Newport, RI, we were transported by boat to Quonset Point NAS for two years of land duty followed by two years of sea duty.

My US Navy days before Laura and I were married.

We were assigned temporary quarters and reported to classes to determine how we could best serve the navy. My test results suggested I be an Admiral's assistant, which I refused. Instead, I accepted a position as an aviation store keeper in the supply department. Jim was assigned to the training unit and operated a simulator, which was a mockup of a plane cockpit.

Jim and I would get together a couple of times a week, watch a movie, have lunch at the canteen, or just hang out together. As time went on and we became proficient in our jobs, I had an opportunity to apply for a job as the base "open purchase agent." Having made friends in high places, I obtained references, interviewed, and got the job.

My two most treasured assets,
my wife Laura and my 1935 Ford.

It was a tough job, but somebody had to do it. I would pick up my truck in transportation, drive to the Supply Office, pick up my vouchers and my box lunch for the day, and travel a 30 to 40 mile radius from the base. My route was primarily in the Providence area. After completing my pickups, I would stop in Roger Williams Park and have my lunch before returning to the base to deliver my orders. Next stop, return my truck to Transportation and call it a day.

One morning, I went to pick up my truck and was asked if I could drive a double clutch flatbed truck. I said sure, it couldn't be that difficult. I was told to take my pickup and go to the supply depot and get the pickup orders and return to transportation and pick up the flatbed. I did what I was told and jumped into the flatbed and headed for Providence. I had never driven such a huge truck and would stop and start from time to time to practice the double clutching and stick shift combination. A plate on the dashboard provided the shifting instructions, so it seemed like no big deal. Arriving at the warehouse, I was told to back up to the loading platform between two trailers. Somehow I knew how to use the large mirrors on both doors to guide me as I backed up, mission accomplished. A fork lift put pallets of floor tiles on the flatbed which were secured with strapping. The documents were signed and I was ready to return to the base. To my surprise, as I pulled away from the platform, the weight of my load totally changed the driving experience compared to an empty truck. I drove all the way back in second and third gear, down shifting prior to stopping at a light. God must have been my co-pilot, for to this day, I don't know how I did it. I made the delivery at the base and returned the truck to Transportation. Another day, another experience, and a lesson learned that I can do it until it is proven that I can't, and with God everything is possible.

I was driving to Providence with my pickup truck and a fellow was hitch hiking on the side of the road, so I stopped and picked him up. After a spell of small talk, he told me that he was getting married shortly. I asked him when and he replied, "October 13, and I am getting married by a Monsignor." "Is that a fact?" I said. "We are also getting married on the same date by a Monsignor." He continued that they were going to New York for their honeymoon and staying at the Hotel Taft. "Is that a coincident or what?" I said. "We are booked at the Taft as well. We will have to get together for a drink." As I dropped him off, he turned and said, "We'll see you in New York in the fall. And by the way, my name is Roger Gilbert and I work at Quonset Point."

Things do happen in strange ways and this was strange.

Chapter 4

Our wedding day

Our wedding day had arrived! It was a beautiful day on October 13, 1952 and a day Laura and I will never forget … but for different reasons.

We had a beautiful wedding mass at Sacred Hearts Church in Bradford, officiated by Monsignor Madden. As Jim and I waited for Laura to enter the church, I can still hear the wedding bands rattling in Jim's pocket. I think Jim was a little nervous. The wedding was followed with a full breakfast at the Cedar Crest Restaurant in Lawrence for the immediate family. That was followed a couple hours later by a full reception at the Bradford Grange.

It was totally a family affair back then, no professional wedding services were needed. Alma, my mother-in-law, did all the cooking. She prepared a main course of spaghetti and meat balls. Lucy and Alice, Laura's sisters, did all the

39

decorations. It was a great day and everyone had a good time. My Uncle Al, who drove the wedding car, couldn't remember having such a good time at a wedding! And, keeping with the family theme, Laura's Uncle Al took the wedding and reception photos.

Couples (L-R) Bob and Dot Amirault; Joe and Alice Abate; John and Laura; Robert S. Amirault; Jim Betournay and Lucy Amirault; Norman Dumas and Carol Marcote.

After the reception, Laura and I changed into our traveling clothes and bid our guests goodbye. My dear mother handed us a box lunch to eat on our way to Boston, our first stop on our way to New York. By this time we were starving so we stopped at the Howard Johnson's parking lot on Route 28 to eat our boxed meal. Laura was wondering what kind of nutty family had she married into.

Our parents (L-R) John B. and Beatrice A. Cartier and
Alma M. and Robert S. Amirault.

The next morning we had breakfast and were off to New York. I was driving on Route 9 in my father's 1939 Dodge, which was in much better shape than my 1935 Ford. I had mentioned to Laura that we were going right by Ashland, where Laura's brother Bob and his wife Dot lived, so we should stop in to say hello. Laura, not wanting to hurt my feelings, agreed. But Laura was still thinking, "What have I gotten myself into if he wants to visit family on our honeymoon? Oh well, it has to get better." We finally arrived at our destination, the Taft Hotel in Times Square.

The happy couple.

I called the Gilberts (remember the hitchhiker I had picked up on my way to Providence?) to tell them we had arrived and invited them for supper. After supper we all went back to our room for a lively game of canasta. Laura was now thinking this really couldn't get any worse! Oh, but it did. The next day I invited the Gilberts for a stroll in Central Park, followed by lunch together. Not a good move on my part. Laura had had enough! We had a little talk, and that was the last of the Gilberts.

Our honeymoon was almost back on track. We ran into Eddy Hashim, an old friend who was an actor living in New York, so we had lunch with him. That was the end of the diversions. The rest of our honeymoon was just Laura and me enjoying our time together as husband and wife.

Our first apartment

About a month before Laura and I got married, I rented a second floor apartment on Chapin Ave in Providence, RI. It seemed like a quiet neighborhood right near the Armory. Jim and I spent several nights cleaning and polishing the apartment so it would look nice for Laura. To my delight, she was very pleased. We moved in with all our stuff and set up housekeeping.

Laura got a job as a secretary at the Iron Foundry close by and I was employed as an open purchase agent at the Quonset Point, Naval Air Station. We liked the apartment except for the shared bathroom with our next door neighbor. It was fairly tolerable. Our neighbors were a young couple and we got along with them well.

As the months passed, the couple next door bought a house and moved out. Two young bachelors took the apartment. The only thing separating us was two small hook latches. That wasn't going to work so I replaced them with two heavy duty sliding bolts. The arrangement seemed to be going well.

Laura and I made frequent weekend trips back home to Haverhill when I wasn't on duty. After one such weekend we noticed that something had gone on in our apartment during our absence. I asked our next door neighbors if they had seen anything and they confirmed that there had been a party in our apartment on Saturday night. I went to our landlord's home and found him working in his yard. When I filled him in on what we confirmed had happened Saturday night, he became furious. He yelled for his teenage son, Mike, to come outside immediately. Mike complied and, as he approached, asked his father what the problem was all about.

"Where were you Saturday night?" his father asked. Mike told him at a party.

"And where was that, Mike?" his father asked.

"At a friend's house," Mike responded.

The landlord grabbed the front of his son's shirt and raised him off the ground saying, "Don't lie to me son or you will pay the consequence."

Mike was shaking as his dad lowered him back down to the ground. He decided to tell his dad the truth and he confessed to having the party in our apartment.

"I want you to apologize to Mr. Cartier and ask him if he would mind if you paid his next month's rent" said his father. I accepted. Mike never came near our apartment again.

Some months later during a July heat wave, our windows were open and we were awakened by loud noises coming from our next door second floor apartment. The husband was drunk and his wife was tied to a chair while he threatened to kill her. He said after he killed her he was going next door to kill the sailor, which was me.

"That's it Laura," I said, "We're moving out of this nut house." Goodbye Chapin Ave., hello Arizona St.

Next stop Arizona St.

We were fortunate to have found a very small cottage near a lake on Arizona St. in Coventry, RI. It was closer to the base and it was available for immediate occupancy. We packed the 1935 Ford and moved right in. It was summer and we enjoyed the lake and being in our own cottage.

During one of my explorations of the area, I found another lake further down the road. I talked with a local man who rented boats. Our conversation turned to fishing, which he said was great in this area, and that the lake was loaded with pickerel. He told me where the best spot to catch these beauties was and he was dead on. Each time I rowed to this certain spot I would get a strike on my faithful dare devil. After a good fight, I'd bring up a 16" to 20" fish. My father-in-law, Bob, loved to fish! It didn't take much coaxing to have him fish with me there. On one particular fishing day, with fish in tow, he returned back to our cottage and told his wife, Alma, "That was the best fishing trip I've ever had."

It was a great summer on Arizona St. but there was one important feature we had overlooked when we rented this cottage. There was no heating system. The kitchen stove, which had a heating unit, was our only source of heat. It was okay when it was just Laura and me but when Jackie came along, it was a different story. During the winter months, after returning from a weekend back home, Laura would remain in the car with Jackie while I fired up the stove. Once the inside temperature was acceptable, I would bring Laura and Jackie into the cottage. We only spent one winter on

Arizona St. The summers were great but the winters were difficult.

Laura had mentioned that I had less than one year of active duty left. Therefore, she wanted to take Jackie and move back to Haverhill. Even though I hated to think of losing them for even a moment, I agreed that we should do what was best for both of them. This ended our experience living in Rhode Island together and I moved back to the barracks on base.

Laura's trip to the hospital

When our first child Jackie came into the world at Quonset Point, Naval Air Station, Laura said that she would never go back there for any reason whatsoever, and she meant it, and I agreed. Unfortunately, Laura was having a miscarriage and she had to be taken to a hospital. After checking the list in the telephone book, I had Laura pick out the one she wanted to go to. We left Jackie with friends as Laura and I went to Kent County Hospital in Warwick, RI.

Upon arrival, we filled out all the necessary paperwork and Laura was placed in the emergency room area for examination. The staff was professional and very accommodating. After being assigned a room and awaiting the doctor who would assist us, we settled in and talked about our situation.

The doctor arrived and laid out the procedure and said that Laura would be staying overnight. She would be released from the hospital the following morning around 11:00 AM, as long as all went according to plan. Laura was concerned about Jackie and she suggested that I leave and pick him up. All went just fine, Jackie was no problem, the procedure went according to plan, and Laura was ready to leave the hospital on time.

When I presented the discharge paperwork to the office clerk, she said that we owed them $250.00. As I prepared to make out a check, the clerk told me that all military personnel had to pay in cash only. Credit was not available to the military per hospital policy. I then inquired why this wasn't mentioned to me at admission so I could make necessary arrangements for the cash. I told Laura to remain right there in the waiting room until I returned. I flew out of the hospital in a rage heading to my only hope, my best friend Jim. I sped to the base, found Jim and we headed to the base credit union. In less than five minutes I was heading back to the hospital with cash in hand as well as a chip on my shoulder. As I traveled back to the hospital, I realized that I shouldn't make a scene and get Laura all upset. I entered the waiting room with a smile on my face and gave her a thumbs up. Laura, with an at-a-boy expression and a smile on her face, was now happy I made it back so quickly.

I paid the bill in cash, helped Laura to the car, picked up Jackie at the Hartzells and we went back to Arizona St. together as a family.

But why not Bradford?

We found a nice apartment on Main St. in Haverhill which had a heating system, its own outside entrance, and its own parking space. What more could we ask for? It only needed some sprucing up.

My sister Claire's husband, Norman, and Laura's brother, Bob, pitched in to get the job done. I felt very comfortable about Laura and Jackie living in that apartment. They were close to family. Still, Laura would have preferred that it was in Bradford.

After living there for a few months, I don't remember the reason, but Laura had to make a call. We did not have a phone, so she entered the front door of the apartment building and knocked on the first door to see if she could use their phone. The door opened and a scantily clad middle-aged woman invited her to come in.

"Come on in, honey! What can we do for you?" the woman asked.

Laura stood, shocked, never knowing that for all these months she was living in a house of ill repute. Since our apartment had a private entrance from the outside, Laura was never aware of the activity going on in other parts of the building. Laura couldn't wait for me to get home for the weekend so we could discuss what to do about it. I told Laura that in a couple of months I'd be home for good and I would get a job and we would get our own place. Since she had felt very safe there, we decided she and Jackie would stay for the final few months.

Chapter 5

Is there a sign on my back?

Laura and Jackie were all settled in on Main St. in Haverhill. I was thankful that Laura had family all around her to provide support until I got discharged, which was in approximately six more months. As for myself, I was back at the base and doing my job in the supply department at VC-12. We were located in a huge hangar where a squadron of radar planes was parked next to a large area of tarmac at the edge of Narragansett Bay.

A series of large Quonset huts were located along the bay side of the hangar which housed all the departments that supported the hanger. The supply department was one of these huts.

Around midsummer, the forecast was predicting a major hurricane in our area. After securing the planes with double tie downs, we awaited the storm. It was a beauty. The water rose as we occupied our duty station in the hut.

The water was up to our waist. At this point we got the word to vacate to the hanger and go up to the second level away from the rising water. When the water receded, the damage was minor with one exception; my car had been flooded with water just above the seats.

I cleaned and rebuilt the logical engine parts but when I turned the key, it wouldn't start. I removed the muffler and found it full of seaweed. Once the seaweed was removed, the car started running again. Unfortunately, a year later, all the salt water took its toll and the car died.

Another incident occurred one late afternoon when I was resting on my bunk in the barracks. I heard a sailor yelling, "I'm going to kill him." A couple of sailors near him asked, "Who are you going to kill?" He replied, "That sailor at the other end of the barracks, his name is Cartier." Since I was the only one with that name, I assumed that he was going to kill me. While some of my comrades were trying to restrain him, one of the sailors called the MPS (Military Police), who arrived momentarily. I did the only thing I could think of; I played dead through the whole ordeal. MPS placed him in a straitjacket, removed him from the barracks, and he was never seen again. The strange thing was that we never had an altercation of any kind. When everything settled down and the barracks were quiet once more, I asked another sailor, "Please do me a favor and see if there is a sign on my back."

A strange remark

As my discharge from the navy drew near, my thoughts were consumed with how I was going to support my family. Jim would be going to work for his father in the wood heel factory but I had no idea which direction to go to support my wife and child. God works in strange ways but I wasn't aware of how God would play an important part in our destiny. Two months before we got discharged, the chief of the supply dept. in VC-12 held a party at his home and invited all those leaving the service for a good luck send off. We all had a great time and, when it was time to leave, the chief stood at the door shaking hands with all of us and wishing us all good luck on our future endeavors. When he came to me we shook hands and the chief said, "John, I'm not going to wish you good luck because you are going to create your own good luck." I thanked him for the party and for his remarks, and for our association together. I had no idea what his remark meant, but was enlightened to some extent as life went on and I became consumed with raising our family of seven, which I called "the 7 C's."

Two week trial

My dad worked in a grocery store in Lafayette Square. He happened to be chatting with Mr. Phaneuf, the owner of an insurance company, whose office was in the same square. Mr. Phaneuf said to my dad that Bunny Lagasse, who owned the Lagasse Furniture Co. on Hale Street, was looking for someone to run his office. Would Johnny be interested in applying? I immediately went in to see Mr. Lagasse. His response to me was, "I have had so much trouble with office help, I'm leaving the task of hiring the right person to my accountant, sorry." I returned the next week to ask if the position had been filled. It hadn't. On my third visit, I put a game plan together and presented the following proposition to Mr. Lagasse. "I have two weeks leave still on the books, so I'll use it to come work for you, without pay. You then present my performance to your accountant and if he is satisfied, I get the job. You need someone to cover the position right now, so what do you have to lose? I will be discharged in four weeks and will report for work the following day." With a smile on his face, he asked me if I could deliver several accounting procedures. Not fully understanding what he was talking about, I told him "Of course I can!" We shook hands and he told me to report to work in two weeks. Back at the base I immediately drew two books from the library, one on accounting, the other on basic bookkeeping. I committed every minute of free time to my studies. I was on a mission and I was going to succeed at this job. I reported to work with the two books under my arm. The two weeks passed very quickly. My performance was accepted by the accountant. He told Mr. Lagasse to keep me. Not only did I get the job; but I was paid $1.00 per hour for the two week trial. My office assistant job at American Grocery Co. sure came in handy!

Bradford is nice!

My folks never owned their own home. They always rented and were happy not having the worries of home ownership. I, however, wanted my own house to raise our children. In November of 1955, Laura and I bought our first house on Haseltine St. in the Bradford part of Haverhill. That was an issue between my wife Laura and me, since she was born and had grown up in Bradford, and I was born and had grown up in the French district of Haverhill.

Bradford was considered the elite part of town. When we got married, Laura told me, "I'll follow you wherever you want to go, as long as it's in Bradford." We have lived here all our married life and I have no regrets. I worked seven days a week and I received several raises early on. I knew what I was doing, I was very professional and I gave my job 100%, which is my formula for success. I taught this to all our children and it has worked.

A lesson learned

I learned a great lesson in the process of buying our first house. It was a cute three bedroom, one bath colonial on a very nice kid friendly street. Prior to closing, the seller asked me if they could stay in the house for thirty days while their new home had a new kitchen installed. He said that he would pay rent for his time in my new house. Understanding his dilemma, I agreed to let them stay for thirty days but not a day more because we were anxious to get into our new home. We closed on the house! Now we had both a mortgage and rent to pay on our apartment. As agreed, I went to our new house to collect the rent. He smiled and said, "I'm not paying you a cent because it's the law that a seller can remain on the property for thirty days after closing." My reply was, "But we agreed and we shook hands on it!" He said, "That's right but it wasn't in writing, so it isn't legal." I told him that I would be here thirty-one days from the closing with a moving truck, so you better be gone! Jim and I arrived early on the thirty-first day with the truck. As we entered the front door, the past owner was exiting the back door. I will never forget that experience. That bit of knowledge has served me well over my lifetime.

Education

Getting an education was very important to me in providing for my family and moving forward with my career. Fortunately, I got to go to college under the GI bill. Jim and I enrolled at Merrimack College together attending their night classes. The college was very small with several class rooms and one brick administration building. We both declared business as our major and I took accounting as my minor. By the end of our first year, Jim's small lumber yard was growing and consuming more of his time so he decided to drop out of college. I was working sixty hours a week at Lagassee Furniture but continued to carry one or two subjects per semester. I stayed up nights studying and graduated in 1963 with an associate's degree in accounting. This was a major accomplishment considering my hectic schedule and growing family. Jim continued to work expanding his company which resulted in a very successful business.

The 7 C'S

Jack was born on March 8, 1954 at Quonset Point NAS in Rhode Island. Unfortunately, for him, he was the oldest child and he would set the example for his four siblings; not an easy task in the 60's and 70's in the age of rebellion.

Next came Becky, born November 4, 1956. Both mother and child came down with jaundice and were confined in isolation for two weeks.

The third new comer was Marie, born May 17, 1958, very, very early in the morning. Back then the fathers remained in a special waiting room awaiting the news. I was the only father in the room at the time when I was presented with an infant with bright red hair. I told the nurse to go back and get mine because this baby couldn't possibly belong to us;

Laura and I both had black hair. The nurse returned telling me that it has to be mine, there were no other births in the delivery room. So we had to keep her! This created a detailed investigation into the source of her red hair. It seems that both sides had red hair. My great grandfather on my dad's side was actually known as "Pepere Rouge!"

At the Beginning.
(L-R) Peter, Paul, Marie, Becky and Jack

Marie was followed by Paul, born July 7, 1960. Paul was the forgotten child. Two days after Paul's birth Laura had still not been seen by her doctor. The nurses didn't call so I called the delivering doctor and told him who I was. His response was, "Hi John, how's Laura?" I responded, "She is just fine but she has been waiting for two days for you to see her and the baby." A total silence prevailed. "Oh my God, John, I forgot all about her. I'm so sorry. I'll leave immediately to see her, and listen John, there will be no charge for the circumcision."

Portrait for our Fiftieth Wedding Anniversary.
Back (L-R) Peter and Paul
Front (L-R) Becky, Jack and Marie

Last, but not the least, came Peter. Born April 5, 1961, he just didn't want to start life on time so he had to be induced. He also had red hair but not quite as bright as Marie's, so we kept him without question. At twenty-nine we were the parents of five children in seven years, may God give us strength! Well, before we were married, Laura and I discussed children and we both agreed that we would have seven. Five children should be easy! Laura was the heart of the family and I was the provider and the enforcer.

Chapter 6

Time for a larger nest

Since we had no room for a crib for Peter, we put him in the bottom drawer of our bureau, and yes, we left the drawer open! But this arrangement was certainly not going to work long term. So Laura and I decided that a move to a larger house was an immediate necessity.

Our current house was on Haseltine St in Bradford. It was a quiet street close to convenience stores, schools, family and what would end up being lifetime friends. We paid $9,500 for it back in 1955 and I made a number of improvements to it in the seven years we lived there. We loved this house and the location but we had outgrown it!

Shortly after our decision to look into a larger house, I was walking to my in-laws home at 522 South Main St., when I spotted a recently placed "for sale" sign on the front lawn at 466 South Main St. It was a gorgeous house on a half acre of land. I got very excited, it would be perfect for us. I ran back home to tell Laura. She knew the house and immediately said that we couldn't possibly afford it, and that it was surely out of our price range.

The Little House — 1955 to 1962.

"Let's just look at it," I said. I called the real estate office listed on the sign and made an appointment to view it. We went, saw it, and loved it! It had four large bedrooms with walk-in closets, 1 and a half bathrooms, a twenty foot long kitchen, a huge laundry room and a cold storage room. It listed for $21,500, I offered $15,000, and we compromised at

$16,500. We lived there raising our family for thirty-three years!

The Big House – 1962 to 1995

Now we had to quickly sell our house on Haseltine St. I told our agent, John Furlong, "Sell it for what you can get, I want to take away $13,500, the balance is your commission." John agreed, we shook on it and I told him to put it in writing. He said, "Not necessary." I was not about to make the same mistake twice! He put our agreement in writing. Unfortunately, John Furlong passed away ten days later from a heart attack. I hope my transaction didn't contribute to his demise. Laura and I felt terrible but we had to move forward with the house sale.

The first person to view our house was the wife of a retiring engineer from Chicago. She found fault with every detail of the house. I told Laura, "She will never buy it." Actually, she DID buy it, and for full asking price! Sometimes, it's really hard to read people.

Once I told the real estate office of my arrangement with John Furlong, the sale contract was accepted but the attorneys just couldn't get the transaction details right. It took three contract renditions before I could accept and sign. Next was to coordinate the closings of both properties on the same day. Amazingly, the transactions went according to schedule.

Marching orders

Moving into our new house, with five kids in tow, required major organization! In order to avoid chaos, rules and duties were established for each child according to age and gender. They all had to make their own beds, pick up their rooms, and put their clothes in the hamper. Other duties such as dishes, cleaning, and mowing the lawn were more specific to their ages. Jack, the oldest, was having difficulty conforming to one of the rules, putting things where they belong. Jack asked, "Ma, where are my shoes and pants?" Laura answered, "I don't know, why don't you ask your father?" I replied, "You left your clothes on the floor too many times, you don't seem to care, so I threw them out in the trash." Jack rushed down to the cellar and searched the waste barrel until he found his lost items. Funny, it never happened again!

Our first camping trip

Peter was around two years old when we went on our first camping excursion to Bear Brook campground in NH. Our good friends, the Josephson's, had lent us their large tent along with camping accessories. We packed our station wagon and away we went! The kids were all excited and ready for the long Memorial weekend adventure of swimming, hiking and camp fires.

The weather was perfect when we arrived at the campsite. Our camp neighbors saw that we were novices and pitched in to help us erect the canvas monster. As the night approached it got cooler and cooler. Having little protection against the cold other than the papers under us and our sweaters and jackets, we had difficulty falling asleep, so we spent most of the night laughing and telling stupid jokes.

Morning slowly arrived around 6 am. I started a fire so we could all warm up. I hung a mirror on a tree so I could wash and shave, the water was freezing, shaving cream was freezing and there I am in 40° weather with my razor shaving. I'm thinking, this is nuts coming out into the wilderness to be miserable! This was followed by a breakfast of cold cereal and bananas. And let's also mention the long lines at the bathroom! Well, I'm thinking, let's make the best of it. And we did! The kids had a blast swimming in the lake and playing at the nearby playground. The weekend turned out to be great fun and the first of many camping trips to come!

Life is good / Lagasse Furniture

We loved our new big house and the kids were growing like weeds. I would leave the car for Laura once a week so she could go grocery shopping with all five kids. Laura never complained!

I finally graduated from Merrimack College after eight years of night classes. You would think that after all that time I would be getting a bachelor's degree but since I felt it important to maximize my time at home with the family, I limited my class load to one or two subjects a semester. In 1963, I settled with an associate's degree with a B+ average. I had the best of both worlds, my family and my profession.

Hard at work in my office at Lagasse – Brentwood.

I was well established as the office manager of Lagasse Furniture. They produced furniture wood frames and Brentwood Furniture produced the upholstered finished product. The Lagasse Furniture name was eventually dropped and the operations were merged into one company, Brentwood Furniture. As the company grew to 220 employees, we bought the building across the street and utilized the total second floor for office space and a large conference room for sales meetings.

I stole Lucy, my sister-in-law, from H.L. Green department store where she worked as office manager, to work as our HR manager. Later, I recruited Laura's other sister, Alice, to work in our order entry department.

I chose to give my time to a smaller company so I could be involved with all the functions within the company. I loved the challenge and enjoyed the multi-tasking required to cover all phases of the business. I loved my job, and yes, I needed to provide for my family, which this position allowed me to do. It's one thing to obtain and another thing to sustain.

Several years after joining Brentwood Furniture, I recommended we improve clerical and production efficiencies by purchasing a computer. They eventually agreed and were counting on me to make the computer an asset rather than a liability for the company. I was put to the test and applied my life long philosophy "I can do it until it's proven that I can't." Applying my God given talent to analyze and solve problems, I did research and found the best computer for our needs. Now I needed a reliable software programmer to work with me. I approached a professor at Northern Essex Community College, Barry Carver, who was teaching computer programming. He agreed to work with me on weekends. He taught me programming and I taught him manufacturing. I formulated my objectives and we sat side by side developing the software system. Not only were we a great team, we became close friends in the process. We put the system under major testing to debug errors and guarantee a smooth transition from the manual process to the automated process. It was flawless and received accolades from the owners as well as the users.

A short time after the successful computer installation, Mr. Lagasse called me into his office and told me to run over to Smith Chevrolet and pick out a new car and also apply for a company credit card. Mr. Lagasse, whose nickname was Bunny, would frequently slip me a $50 bill and tell me to take Laura out for a nice meal – his way of thanking me for all my extra effort. We had made it, I considered us affluent! I had successfully reached my goals with a great family, a nice home, two cars, a profession that was a daily challenge which I enjoyed every minute of, and a strong faith in God who provided me with the necessary gifts to succeed. But wait, this might have been the fulfillment of my life's ambitions but there were changes on the horizon that I did not expect.

To Florida in the new wagon

When Peter, the youngest, was about four, we decided to try out the new station wagon and the second hand pop-up trailer and take a trip to Florida to visit my sister, Claire, and her husband, Norman, in Sarasota. We packed our custom carrier drawers with clothing and emergency tools, I attached my homemade storage unit to the wagon roof, filled the gas tank (using the company credit card as ordered by Bunny) and, with the trailer in tow and our AAA tour guide in hand, we set off for Florida!

Our first overnight stop was a huge camping area on the outskirts of Washington, D.C. As we were driving to our camping site, Laura spotted a woman she knew from Haverhill. I told her, "You know, Laura, we see a lot of people who look like someone we know when it isn't really them." She came back, "I know it is her and I'm going to run over to see her." Well, Laura was right! The odds were not in her favor but she was right! It's a small world.

We got back to our site after meeting the woman from Haverhill and did a head count. Last I knew we had five kids but the head count was only four. Peter was missing! We immediately started searching for him, arranging to meet back

71

at our campsite in ten minutes, site #522. We spread the word as we travelled through the different streets until we finally found him, happily talking to campers. His opening remark to us was, "I'm not lost, I know where I am all the time." I suppose there is some logic to his remark; the confidence of a four year old!

After breakfast the next morning we were back on the road. I couldn't find our next destination camp site, I drove past it, so I kept driving into the night. We arrived at the following destination site around 6:30 AM. Unfortunately, we had to wait until they opened at 7:00 AM to register.

We got our site and set up the pop-up trailer, had the kids put on their bathing suits, and we ran into the water! Did I mention this was in July and the water temperature was around 80 degrees? Nobody should go to Florida in July, at least not with five children and a camper. Becky, age nine, asked, "Dad, why did we have to go so far for a vacation?" "To visit family," I said. We arrived in Sarasota in a heat wave. Peter immediately fell asleep for hours and Laura was under the weather for a couple of days. Otherwise, we had a pleasant visit with my dear sister and her husband.

On our trip back home we stopped at a family camping area that was referenced in my AAA tour guide. We were refused entry because we had children, which they didn't allow. I told them that this would be reported to the AAA for misrepresentation, which I did and AAA investigated the issue.

Unfortunately, we ended up sleeping in a gas station parking lot that night. The remaining trip home, I am happy to say, was uneventful.

Chapter 7

At North Salisbury beach

Tomorrow was supposed to be an exceptionally nice day and the kids would all be in school so I took the day off. Laura packed a lunch and I packed the car with total efficiency. I had plenty of time to double check and be sure we had everything we needed for a wonderful day at the beach, just the two of us. Other people seemed to have had the same idea, parking spaces were scarce, and the sand was covered with bodies of all shapes and sizes. However, we did find a spot sufficient to set up our chairs, and all was well. We removed our outer garments since we had our bathing suits on underneath. I folded my clothes very neatly along with Laura's and all of a sudden Laura yelled, "JOHN, YOU DON'T HAVE YOUR BATHING SUIT ON," which could be heard within a fifty yard radius. All eyes were on me standing there in my BVDs. The woman behind us was outraged. She gathered up her belongings and three young children and left to find better ground away from this nut.

Do you have any idea how long it takes to find your pants and put them on while on your knees? It seemed like an eternity as I, "Mr. Efficient," attempted to put my pants back on while hundreds of laughing spectators watched. As I finished dressing, I got up, bowed and sat in my chair. The laughter quieted down and life returned to normal once again. To this day I still get cards, drawings and remarks about my day at the beach from my supposedly best friends. My reply to all this is, "Nobody is perfect." Another lesson learned is to never lose your sense of humor.

Actions speak louder than words

Sheila, who happened to be a school mate of Laura's, lived next door to us. Her house was about ten feet from our driveway. Sheila was divorced and lived there with her daughter, mother and aunt. She was high maintenance when it came to her minor home repairs. I was appointed, by majority vote, to be their permanent handy man and Sheila was the permanent task master. I agreed to help out if I was available. Unfortunately, things got out of hand and I was spending more and more time helping out the poor ladies next door. One Saturday afternoon I was out washing the cars when suddenly Sheila's kitchen window opened and she started to mention she needed my help with a home project. For some unknown reason my right hand went up, which happened to be holding a hose, and I sprayed Sheila dead center through the open window. The kitchen window quickly came down. How does the saying go? Actions speak louder than words. One good thing was that we both seemed to have a strange sense of humor, and Sheila took it all in stride. I did apologize for my bad behavior. This was an occasion which was forgiven but not forgotten. Sheila would often ask at numerous gatherings, "Did I ever tell you what John did to me?"

A fence makes good neighbors

We had been going on family camping trips since the children were small. For a short time (thank goodness) we had five teenagers and going on family camping trips was not on their agenda. So, what should we parents do to retain our family unit? We sold our twenty foot trailer that slept eight, the boat, and all the water skiing equipment, and took down two trees. With the help of a friend's tractor, which had a hole digger attached, I was able to dig 58 post holes and install a six foot stockade fence around the complete back yard which was just shy of a half-acre. Next we had a 20'x40' in-ground pool installed with the help of Harvey Lumber's pool installers. The pool wouldn't be complete without a six foot apron and a platform to build a 20'x20' sun room which I designed and built myself. We landscaped the whole yard, complete with new grass and loads of flowers and bushes. Our house became the cool place for our children and friends to come and hang out. Our summer's hosted gatherings of forty to fifty people enjoying the pool, playing horse shoes, badminton, ping pong, and card games.

All was well in paradise, with one exception; good friends of ours lived on Fernwood Ave. and our back yards were now separated by a six foot fence. Marilyn, our neighbor, was insulted and very angry, "How dare the Cartier's put up a ten foot fence in our back yard." I told her it wasn't a ten foot fence but a six foot fence and I put a gate in that section so her family could come over to use the pool. I informed her that it's the law that all in-ground pools were required to be fenced in. For thirty years she would remark about the fence whenever we met. Nothing is forever on this earth and many years later Marilyn's husband passed away. Being good neighbors we attended the wake. As I stood face to face with Marilyn she gave me a big hug, kissed me on the cheek and said, "John, I forgive you for installing the ten foot fence." "Glad to hear that, Marilyn, for John (her husband) is at peace and I hope you are as well." Could she have misinterpreted that remark? I hope not.

And now the left side neighbors

As the saying goes, "Love thy neighbor as thyself." We did that for the most part but there are always those times when we are tested and fall short of our Christian obligations. This story involves an elderly couple who lived in the house to our left. The husband was the basketball coach for the local high school and his wife was the Haverhill chairperson for a political party. He was a gentle person, unlike his wife, who was very loud and controlling. The husband was slightly built and his wife was somewhat different in size.

Since the neighbors on the right were in need of assistance from time to time, why shouldn't our neighbors on the left also be in need of our assistance? So I made myself available to them, which was most appreciated by one of them. Laura would say, "John, don't push yourself too hard helping everyone in need." Being the only ones with a snow blower, we cleared the snow on the right, center and left side of our house, and the boys took care of the sidewalks and steps. One snowy day, Mrs. Left side neighbor came running out, yelling as usual, and told Peter that he didn't make the opening for the oil man wide enough. She instructed him to make it wider, turned around, and marched back into the house. Peter looked at me and said that he was going to shovel the snow back. I told him to just widen the path and offer it up since two wrongs don't make it right. He reluctantly complied.

Another time, Mrs. Left side neighbor approached me to advise me that I shouldn't park in front of my house anymore because "I can't see as I back out of my driveway." My reply was, "Why don't you just cut down the overgrown bushes at the end of your driveway (which stood about eight feet tall) then you will be able to see?" She replied, "Never will I touch those bushes, they are living things." I replied, "Then just cut them down to four feet and your problem will be solved." She replied, "So you're telling me that it's okay for your visitors to park in front of your house." "I think that that would be fair to assume," I said. She went in the house in a huff. A week passed and Laura called me at work to tell me that a "No Parking" sign was being erected in front of our house by the highway department. I told her that I would be right there. When I got home the sign was up and the men were gone. I immediately visited the mayor at City Hall and presented my case about having the sign removed. The mayor said, "Do you know how it is dealing with a person like her? She is impossible to reason with." I replied, "Yes, Mayor, I live right next door and deal with it on a daily basis." The mayor said that if he didn't put up the sign, he wouldn't have a day's rest. At that point, I replied, "Mr. Mayor, if the sign doesn't come down, I assure you that a day's rest would be a thing of the past. I will see to it that there will be no parking for the full length of South Main St. and on both sides." In the end, the mayor conceded and told me to take the sign down, but requested that I not tell her who it was that told me to, or she would be on his back again. The sign came down and the bushes stayed up.

An act of charity

It was around 8:30 PM when we returned from a weekend camping trip. I had just backed the trailer up the driveway and was bringing the perishables into the house when the telephone rang.

"Hello, John, this is your left side neighbor, we have a major problem that needs to be resolved immediately."

"And what could that be?" I replied.

"Our two grandchildren are stranded in a field over in Andover with a horse and trailer. Our daughter never came to pick them up. It's dark and they are scared silly, could you possibly go and get them?" Although I was tired, with directions in hand, I took off to rescue their grandchildren.

Upon arrival at the field, with my car lights on high beam, I located the trailer and the two kids. They were cold and scared. They had a lantern but no lighter. I got the lantern lit and backed up to the horse trailer.

The wiring was not compatible to mine so the grandson traveled in the trailer holding the lantern. His sister rode in the car with me. This did not exactly follow the code of law as you could imagine. By some act of faith, we made it back to Haverhill without incident. It was now around 10:30

or so as I pulled into the driveway on Lake St., the kid's home. The house light went on and their mother opened the door and yelled to them to get the horse bedded and then get in the house immediately. She then slammed the door shut. I remained with the kids until their chores were done and they ran safely into their house. I then drove back home.

Upon arriving home, Laura acknowledged how long I was gone and checked that everything went okay. I replied, "Yes dear, we all got home safely and I'll give you the details in the morning." I kissed her good night and we went to bed.

A knock at the door

"Can someone answer the back door please?" It was the right side neighbor, Sheila, and her daughter Liz. They came in smiling and, after serving them a cup of coffee, they proceeded to ask us a favor.

Sheila began, "Liz is engaged and they would like to have their wedding in your back yard." I replied, "Well, that is interesting, how many guests would you expect to have?" Sheila said, "About 100 to 150!"

"Tell us, what would be your game plan and when would this blessed event occur?" I asked.

"This summer. We would have a large tent to serve the catered meal, which would be prepared in your kitchen, a DJ, and a platform for dancing. The wedding would take place in front of the fence at the horseshoe pit, and we will have white chairs in a semi-circle to witness the ceremony. Our wedding song will be Feeling Groovy.

"So you seem to have it all taken care of, with two exceptions. What if it rains, and will you have parking attendants?" I went on to say, "This is all too much to make a quick decision, it's not a yes or a no, we will talk about it and let you know our decision."

We agreed. We had the wedding in our backyard! It was a huge success, the weather was perfect, and a good time was had by all! But our back yard would not be the site of any future weddings.

Chapter 8

Our many weekends in New York City

Auntie Lu, Laura's sister, never married. She treated all her nieces and nephews as if they were her own. This was great for us because she would think nothing of giving us an occasional weekend escape to New York City.

The weekend would go something like this: We would hop a plane on Friday afternoon from Logan, check in at the Taft Hotel, and after a quick lunch we'd be off to the play South Pacific. Then we would sleep in Saturday morning, eat a late breakfast and hit the Radio City Music Hall for the matinee. After that we would take a short walk to Times Square for a Reuben sandwich at the Deli, in remembrance of our honeymoon, but this time just the two of us.

Sunday morning we would get up early and walk down to Times Square to breakfast in a unique restaurant. The cooks would take our order, fry it in a pan, and serve it to us in the same pan. After breakfast, weather permitting, we would walk to St. Patrick's Cathedral to attend Mass. Then we would go back to the Taft Hotel, grab a bite, pick up our luggage, check out, take a cab to the airport, and fly back to Logan. Finally, we would jump in our car and arrive home by late Sunday afternoon.

We could hear the kids yelling, "Mom and Dad are home," and we would be met at the door by five laughing children and a smiling Auntie Lu. After giving everyone their little remembrance from the Big Apple, it was story time. First we would give them a detailed account of our weekend. Then all five kids would tell us what they had done for the last two days.

They had been on a nature walk, gone bowling, visited this one or that one, went to the 9:00 AM Mass, and filled their stomachs with Auntie Lu's great cooking. As an end note, Auntie Lu loved to spoil the children, but she was very strict and protected them from any activity that might cause them injury. We would all have a good time and life would go back to normal with the 7 C's.

Wouldn't it be nice if every family had an Auntie Lu? How blessed we were to have her.

Come on Marie, it will be fun

Becky was a junior and Marie was a freshman at Haverhill High School. The drama class was going to put on the play Once Upon a Mattress, which had featured Carol Burnett. Becky was sure she would get a good part but didn't want to go alone to the audition. She wanted Marie to go with her. After much coaxing, Marie reluctantly agreed to go but didn't want to be in the play. Audition day arrived and off they went. Becky was all excited as she tried out for a lead part. Marie was asked what part she would like to try out for and she replied the one that Carol Burnett played. The next day the results were posted on the bulletin board and Becky was in the chorus and yes, Marie had the lead part. It was a huge success and a big party was scheduled after the third night show. I wasn't that happy about our freshman daughter being out at a party with a bunch of juniors without her older sister. However, I did feel that Marie could handle any situation that might arise. I sat up until two in the morning, way beyond curfew, waiting for her to come home. When she didn't, I went to the party house looking for her. As I was searching from room to room the whole house got quiet and I heard them saying in a whisper, "I think that's Marie's father." They directed me to the kitchen where she was still riding high on her theatrical accomplishments that evening. "Come Marie, the party is over." We left without incident and the consequences were extra duties for breaking curfew.

John, you must be strong for me

Another first in our married life was when our oldest son, Jack, was about to be married and leaving the nest. A happy occasion and just another cycle of life, I label it as "bitter sweet." Was I losing a son or gaining a daughter? The wedding was taking place at Star of the Sea church in Salisbury. As Laura and I were traveling north on Route 495, Laura turned to me and said, "John, you must be strong for me." Yes, my dear, not to worry. I, in my tux and patent leather shoes, full of confidence, and in control at all times, put the mother of the groom at ease. As the church was filling up, corsage attached to Laura's gown and lapel flower on my tux, we were escorted down the aisle by our son, Peter, and directed to the front row. No sweat, everything was under control and on schedule. The wedding was beautiful and the newlyweds held hands, and with huge smiles, were greeting everyone along the way out. Linda, the bride, looked beautiful and Jack looked handsome. The ceremony was over, pictures were taken and the receiving line was formed. The parents of the bride first, followed by the bride and groom, and the parents of the groom bringing up the rear.

As the guests started down the line with the usual greetings, handshakes, and hugs, I could feel my emotions taking control of my entire body and the loudest sobbing came pouring out of me. All eyes focused on me as Laura stood there, very stately and in full control, trying to console me and stop the damn crying, which was totally impossible. As the guests approached, not knowing how to address me, they stood there with strange looks on their faces, shook my hand, and marched on. The sobbing continued throughout the whole receiving line event to my total embarrassment. It all passed, jokes were made by the DJ, and we all laughed, including me. I must confess that this spectacle occurred at all five weddings! My family and friends who knew me well knew that I was capable of crying while watching a sad story on the TV, or reading a book. Laura would turn to me with a smile and the expression on her face would say "There goes my strong John again."

High school and band music

Jack had played the guitar in a small group he formed with a few boys from Bradford. Jack didn't have any interest in joining the High School Band. However, Becky, Marie and Paul did! Becky played the oboe, Marie played the saxophone and Paul played the trombone. To help with their band activities, Laura and I joined the BPA (Band Parent's Association) and became active in meetings. Shortly thereafter I assumed the position of the BPA president. We met once a month and became friendly with some of the band parents. A few of these relationships are still close today. We enjoyed our time and efforts with fund raising, socials, and summer music camps at UNH in Dover, NH. Marie, musically talented and being our outgoing child, became the first female Drum Major for Haverhill High School. She led the marching band at parades and directed them on the field at football games. Her sophomore year she actually came out on the field dressed in a large pink elephant costume dancing with the cheerleaders. Marie got attention in so many ways but all in good fun. Becky and Paul played their hearts out at social events and parades. As for Marie, while attending the University of Lowell, she often competed for first chair in the sax section of several ensembles, even though she was a Business Major. Marie would audition and receive first chair all four years of college. Others would come and challenge her for the position, and most of the time she retained her chair. As for Peter, the youngest of the 7Cs, he played a great radio!

A triple play

Throughout our married life, Laura and I have had some very close friends. We had some crazy friends too that always guaranteed a really fun time. One of these groups consisted of our longtime friends Barbara and Bob Girard, and Norma and Roger Goddu. The six of us would often go into Boston for the weekend to catch a play or show. As usual, I would organize the weekend, pre-register at a hotel, order tickets for a play, and arrange other activities for us.

At the start of our very first weekend away together the fun began. While we were on our way to our rooms at the Marriott Hotel in Newton, MA, Roger stepped into a tray full of dishes that were set out in the hallway. This little episode ignited a period of laughter and set the mood for the weekend. After a quick lunch in the dining room, we went back to one of our rooms where we indulged in the contents of our traveling refreshment cases along with a variety of treats which we brought along. The night was spent playing cards, telling jokes, and just plain conversation which was usually about our kids.

Our Boston Trip Group.
Couples (L-R) Bob and Barbara;
Roger and Norma and John and Laura.

One great part about our Boston weekends was that it was close enough for us to return home if there were any problems with our kids. We could be home in less than an hour, so we all took our own cars for just that purpose.

Our NY Trip Group.
Couples (L-R) Laura and John;
Barbara and Bob and Ellen and Frank.

On Saturday morning we all met in the dining room for breakfast, and the talk was about how excited we were to go to the Wilbur Theater that night to see the play Annie live on stage. Unfortunately, Roger's car had broken down in the parking lot that afternoon. As it happened, Roger had the necessary parts at home to solve the problem. I drove Roger back to Haverhill for the parts and back to the parking lot to do the repairs, which proved successful. One small problem still remained: we had left no time for dinner, and we would be late for the play.

I remembered that there was a deli close to the theater, so I told everyone to follow me. We emerged from the deli with three brown bags of sandwiches, pickles and cold drinks. With tickets in hand, and only five minutes late, we took our seats and enjoyed the play immensely. At intermission we opened our bags and had our lunch to the amazement and shock of our surrounding neighbors. We returned back to the hotel with Norma and Barbara sitting together in the third seat of our station wagon and singing in harmony at the top of their lungs, "Tomorrow, tomorrow, the sun will come out tomorrow." To this day, I cannot get that scene out of my mind. What happy times we had together.

Chapter 9

The Square Restaurant (1 of 3)

Strange how things work out. Our two daughters were college bound and our three boys worked with their hands. When Jack graduated from high school he did not know what he wanted to do, so I bought a restaurant for him to work in. It was known as "The Square Restaurant" and was located in Merrimac, MA. The restaurant was previously owned by a Mr. Casey.

Although it was a cute little eatery, it was in need of some TLC. The 7C's went into action and spit shined the place in and out. The windows were gleaming and showcased flower boxes filled with geraniums. We installed a couple of tables in front of the windows and covered them with red and white checkered table clothes. Within a few weeks, the place was ready for business.

The plan was that Jack would work in the kitchen and Laura and her sister, Alice, would work the counter. We were ready to provide service with a smile and good meals for breakfast and lunch. We featured homemade food and were immediately accepted by the locals. The schedule went as follows: Jack got up at 4:00 AM to make the muffins and start the coffee, Laura and Alice got up at 5:00 AM and opened the doors at 6:00 AM, and I prepared the petty cash to start the day. There was only one glitch on the first day; Laura and Alice didn't know how to open the cash register. A quick call home and I was on my way! But before I could get there, a helpful customer provided the magic touch and got the register opened.

After we closed at 2:00 PM, I'd pick up Peter and Paul after school and we would wash the floors and clean the kitchen in preparation for the next day. Laura's other sister, Lucy, came in on Saturday's to bleach all the coffee cups. Once a week Laura's mother, Alma, would make a beautiful homemade soup as the special for the day. It was a favorite! All the regulars would ask, "What's Ma's soup going to be this week?"

My job was to review the day's receipts, record them in the cash ledger, along with the tax distributions, and prepare the petty cash to start the next day. All this would take place after supper. I would go to bed around 11:00 PM and wake up at 4:00 AM, all while working full time at the plant. Becky and Marie filled in on Saturday's and I eventually hired a full time waitress for weekdays.

The restaurant was a great success and the family truly enjoyed working there. However, two major challenges arose. I couldn't keep up the pace and Jack had a girlfriend who was attending college in New York. Jack would leave after closing on Saturday, drive to New York and come home late Sunday night. One time I found him sound asleep on top of the freezer in the basement of the restaurant.

We operated for about a year at this pace. I decided it was time to call a family meeting. We discussed the pros and cons of running the restaurant and we all agreed that it was now time to sell.

Over the past year we had built a great relationship with the townspeople and the restaurant had a good reputation. So, when Mr. Casey heard that we were selling, he immediately bought it back at the price we paid for it one year earlier. Mr. Casey got a great deal, the family loved the experience, and we learned an invaluable lesson about hard work.

Paul's business (2 of 3)

The end of my own professional career was the beginning of many new adventures. Our son Paul and I had already begun preparations for Cartier Furniture Restoring. Thirty days after we signed a rental agreement for a commercial building in Haverhill, we were ready to open our doors for business. We had two tanks built: a bleach tank and a hot stripping tank for doors. We built a cold stripping table for furniture, a water spray booth to clean off the chemicals, and a work station to dismantle and reassemble furniture. Once we were ready for business, we had a grand opening with pictures in the paper, city dignitaries, and many bank executives in attendance.

The business was such a success that we received an overflow of furniture, doors, and kitchen cabinets. I designed a tagging system consisting of a round disc and wire to attach to the items, which included a white stick-on label with the corresponding number that was on the work order in the office.

On the second floor we built a completely sealed spray booth with filtered air intakes and exhaust fan. Paul was our expert refinisher and built a great reputation for his fine work on our customer's treasured items. Paul's wife, Kathryn, contributed to the beautiful results in the refinishing department by wiping down and lightly sanding all the items in the spraying process. They were a great team and the results of their efforts were evident by the happy faces of our customers.

After two years of a successful business, we decided to discontinue operations due to health issues and waste problems. This venture, along with a few others, has been a wonderful life experience.

Pete's turn (3 of 3)

Now that Peter had a few years developing his skills in the upholstery trade working in different shops, it was now time to provide him the opportunity to test the waters by starting his own upholstery business. Laura and I sat down with Peter and asked him if he thought he was ready to try it on his own.

He didn't have to think about it very long. "Better now than never," he said. "What's the plan? I know you have one!"

"The first thing you need to do, Peter, is to measure out the basement and see if it's feasible," I responded. "Do a shop layout. Map out your ceiling lights, electrical outlets, and the space you need for your upholstery and prep bench." Becky's husband, Joe, is an electrician and would be able to take care of the lights and outlets. "You and I will take care of the rest. I'll set up the office, assist in prep work, and do pickup and deliveries with you. So, when do you want to start the process, Peter?"

"How about right now? It sounds like a great idea, let's do it!" I figured we would be up and running in three weeks as American Upholstery. That was the name of the upholstery shop run by Ray Newman and John Dodier, both friends of Peter's. They had recently retired and agreed to let Peter use the business name. To kick start the new venture, we had business cards printed and got clearance from city hall to run the business at 466 South Main St. All went according to schedule.

Peter remained working part time for a few other shops until we took in more of our own customers. Full time work came sooner than expected.

Peter became very accomplished as an expert upholsterer. He was frequently praised by many of his customers. However, several issues became evident early on. Peter consistently underestimated the material and labor costs which effected the profit margins. Peter also had difficulty working by himself. We brought in Bill Wilson, a colleague of Peter's from earlier shops, in the hopes it would keep Peter focused and on task. Although Bill was a decent upholsterer, he was also a great talker and his presence, unfortunately, did not increase their performance. The quality of Peter's work was excellent but working by himself wasn't working. Although Peter's business was successful, he decided to go back to working for other shops where there was interaction with other upholsterers.

Although none of our sons chose to continue their businesses on their own, all three ventures were successful and were great experiences. These endeavors became stepping stones toward each son's future.

Change is in the wind

As I look back on my twenty-five years at Lagasse-Brentwood, I can't help but smile at the opportunity that was provided to me at the hands of Mr. Alphonse Lagasse, known by everyone as "Bunny." He was the founder, president, CEO, and father to all his 220 employees. Bunny's wife, Kitty, was a happy, joyful soul who brought sunshine wherever she went. Their oldest son, Ralph, was the sales manager. He had his mother's personality and served the company well. Unfortunately, being sickly from birth, Ralph passed away at the age of 47. This was a great loss to Bunny, who was never the same after the loss of his son. Charlie, the youngest, was a crackerjack machinist who could fix anything and everything. However, from the first week Charlie was brought in to replace Ralph, Charlie and I were like oil and water. We had conflicting personalities. We tolerated each other and we'll let it go at that.

In addition to being the office manager, comptroller, corporate clerk, and executor of the profit sharing trust, I took a two year night course at Lowell University to become an EMT. I was a first responder to many injuries caused by the dangerous wood working machinery in the plant. I developed quite a practice and established a code call which came over the PA system just like at the hospitals.

In 1973, Bunny passed away, leaving a tremendous void in the company. Charlie took over command and one of the first things he did was to call me into his office. I sat down, and with his wife, Maureen, sitting beside him, he began to relate how much he appreciated my contribution to the success of the company. He told me that it was his father's wish, and Charlie being in full agreement with his dad, he gave me a $5,000 raise, which had been part of Bunny's pay. This was a very emotional moment for me.

I remained in my position for the next seven years helping Charlie the best that I could. This was a gesture of my appreciation for everything that Bunny had done for me through the years. But, in 1980, I resigned from the company and turned in my company car and my company credit card.

Chapter 10

Difficult times

There are situations in life that we wish we could avoid, but they are inevitable. Our parents were growing old and they needed our attention. Simultaneously, our children were growing up and preparing to leave the nest. Together, these events dramatically increased our stress. We had no options but to attack both sides head on and with as much compassion as we could muster up.

Now that my dad could no longer work as a meat cutter, I brought him in as a bed sander operator at the plant. This was great for him, and required no real amount of energy. All went well for several years. Then, in his mid-late 70s, he was having trouble with his eyesight. He also was exhibiting poor judgement driving his car, which resulted in three accidents in just two months. I was faced with the difficult task of taking my dad's independence away from him.

He loved his car and wiped it down every day before putting it in the garage. I called his insurance company to have his license revoked. The insurance rep stated that his insurance would soon be up for renewal and at that time they would send out the notice that his license would not be renewed. Shortly thereafter, a neighbor told me that all the parents in the neighborhood had told their children that when Mr. Cartier was seen backing out of his driveway, they should immediately stop playing in the street and stand on the sidewalk until he passed.

As painful as it was for both of us, it had to be done for the safety of all. Time was now giving evidence of the failing health of both my mom and dad. One day, my mother called to tell me that my dad was out and conditions were icy and she was worried about him because he had been gone for almost an hour. I found him in Washington Square with a bag of Maalox. "You didn't have to come and get me, John. I'm doing just fine," he said. I replied, "But, dad, mom was really worried about your safety."

Mom's health was going downhill as well. She would drink a water sized-glass of wine to soothe the discomfort. Dad had his beer and cigars because he enjoyed them. Mom would call me at all hours because dad was on the floor and he couldn't get up. I would reassure her that I would come right away. I would put him in bed, tuck him in, and give him a kiss on the head. I would kiss my mother too, and would be on my way, until next time.

I could not convince my sisters that our parents needed to be in a nursing home. I was their caregiver and I saw them at their worst. When my sisters came to visit them, they were at their best. I decided to call Dr. Simard and asked him if he would do me a favor. "Would you make a visit to my folk's place unannounced and tell me what you find?" He agreed. He happened to visit them at their worst, called me, and said that they must be in a nursing home immediately. I asked him to please call my sisters and inform them of what he had told me. He did so and my nightmare was finally over. That is, I thought it was.

Forever imbedded in my mind is the two of them walking down the stairs of their second floor apartment, both with their small suitcase containing their personal belongings, for the last time. Has life been reduced to this? Are we doing the right thing for them? Will I ever come to terms with what I have just done to my parents? My sister, Claire, accompanied me with this chore to ease the pain. We got them settled into their nice double room together, gave them a hug and a kiss, and told them that we loved them. As we were departing from the room, our mother followed us out and down the hall yelling and cursing. "How can you do this to us after all we have done for you through the years?" This was definitely one of the saddest moments of my life. And yes, I left the nursing home crying uncontrollably. This was on June 30, 1972. My mother was 78 and my dad was 77 years old.

Life with Mom

My mother, Beatrice, had a bright and playful side as well as a sad side. Her earliest memory of her childhood was when she was nine years old. Her father pinned a money purse to her under-garment and boarded her on a train from Haverhill, MA to Biddeford, ME to cover her mother's funeral expenses. Her mother had died under the care of nuns in a convent. My mother never gave me any other details surrounding this strange trip.

I have a picture of my mother, with a couple of her college friends, clowning around and having fun. They were studying to be nurses. She graduated but was only employed as a nurse for a very short time. Unfortunately, she struggled with her patient's suffering and death.

My mother Beatrice graduating from Nursing School in 1913.

Laura and I and the five kids frequently stopped at my parent's house for bags of popcorn when we were headed on day trips. My mother also set aside every Tuesday to serve me a lunch of sirloin steak and French fries. She didn't spoil me as a kid but she certainly did later!

My mother was quite controlling, even as she was aging. On one of my parent's frequent invites to dinner, my mother asked Marie to sing a song and Marie refused. My mother got very upset and told my father that they were going home "right now!" My mother was strong willed, Marie was strong willed, and I was strong willed. I told my mother to sit back down and had them both apologize to each other. I told my mother that if she still wished to leave after dinner than she could do so. This was the very first time that I had ever stood up to my mother. She realized that the time had come for her to concede to my judgement in future situations. The transition was difficult for both of us but our lives became far more peaceful. A year or so later my mother had a major operation which temporarily affected her memory. She thought I was her father. Over time this symptom passed, but she was never quite the same.

Lesson learned: enjoy the moment – we don't know what tomorrow will bring.

The cycle of life

My mother passed away on March 19, 1978, six years after she and my father entered the Lakeview Nursing Home. It was a rough start, but they soon settled in to a secure and friendly environment. I visited them almost daily.

Once they settled in, I was no longer the bad guy. Mother's Alzheimer's, which was triggered by major surgery in her early seventies, progressed, and Dad's involvement in the daily routine increased over the following six years.

Mother's condition rapidly declined, and her passing was eminent. Our daughter Becky, my sister Jeanne and her husband Don, were on the left side of her bed and I was on the right side holding her hand. My Dad was standing next to me. She died very peacefully. With her strong faith and love for God, and her devotion to His Sacred Heart, I'm sure she had prepared herself for this very moment.

Dad bent toward me and whispered in my ear, "John, I want out of here right now." I replied, "Dad, let's bury Ma first then we will resolve that issue within two weeks, okay?" He agreed and the case closed for the moment. All of the funeral arrangements were made well in advance. There was to be no wake and, per the state law, I was asked to view the body in the casket as the family representative. I entered the funeral home at the designated time with the director present. I couldn't believe my eyes. I had never seen her so beautiful.

She glowed in an amazing peace which I had never seen in my whole life. I asked the director if the family could come in and view this image as a lasting memory of wife and mother. He agreed, and brought them all in to view this remarkable event, which I recall to this day. She was a blessing for all to see.

We had a beautiful Mass at St. Joseph Church, which was full of friends and relatives. I became very emotional and I started crying, totally out of control and very loud, naturally. As this condition was getting worse, I looked way up to the top of the altar, upon which was fixed a dove of peace. The dove was transformed into an image of my mother who looked down on me with a smile and said, "I'm okay Johnny, be at peace." The image disappeared and I immediately stopped crying and became totally at peace for the remainder of the day's activities. It was another unexplainable event which I consider an act of God that came to me in my hour of need. Now that my mother was put to rest, I would turn my attention to my dad and his situation in the nursing home.

Dad's problem solved

Although I visited my dad every day, I told him that I needed more time to iron out the details of his leaving the nursing home. Laura was in favor of whatever my two sisters felt was the best solution, whatever would make dad the happiest for his remaining years. I asked all three women if they would be willing to take dad for four months of the year, and they all agreed. So now I was ready to sit with dad and iron out the details.

I sat face to face with dad at a table in the nursing home. His mind was made up to leave. I began by telling him how many jobs he performed at the home. He locked the doors at night, unlocked them in the morning, ran the bingo games, did the monthly schedule on the blackboard, set up the altar and served Mass for the priest. "And let's face it dad, you do enjoy doing these things and the home really appreciates what you do. Now, that being said dad, I sat down with Laura, Jeanne and Claire and it was agreed by all three that you could stay for four months with each of us. If you would prefer another kind of arrangement, we would all be happy to accommodate your wishes."

I told my dad to think about it for a couple of days or however much time he needed to decide what he would like to do. In the meantime, I spoke to the staff and management about my thoughts on the matter, and I began to feel that Dad's place was right here with his friends and doing his chores. "If you are able to provide him with a private room, I think he would stay. This would be a win-win situation for everyone concerned." Yes, dad decided to stay, and said, "You know John, I'm happy here, I'm secure here and I'm needed here." He had his private room, courtesy of Mr. Guarino, and his friend Charlie, who was also a resident and had a car. They would travel the countryside and so many times they would end up at our house peeking in the sunroom windows to see what activity was going on poolside. They would come in, sit under the big pine tree in the shade with a cold beer and a game of cribbage. Life was good and they made the most of each day.

Dad went home to his wife at age ninety-nine years and four months. We played cribbage thirty days before his death. Every time I would ask him if he wanted another drink, he would always say, "Don't mind if I do." The things you remember! I have been blessed with so many great memories of both Mom and Dad. May they rest in peace together.

My sister Jeanne (1928-1998)

My sister Jeanne was four years older than me. She had a great sense of humor, a hardy laugh, was a prankster, and just enjoyed every moment of life. Upon graduating from high school, she went to work at the Haverhill National Bank as a teller, and soon rose to the position of head teller. When her boyfriend, Donald Surprenant, returned from the Korean War in 1952, they announced their engagement and date of marriage. This was one week before Laura and I announced our date, which was one month after their date. Jeanne and Don married and moved to Danvers, MA, which was closer to his job as an electrician at General Electric in Lynn. Their daughter Donna was born in 1955 and soon after, they adopted their son, Jeff, which rounded out their family. They saw the success that Don's brother, Paul, and his wife, Claire, had buying and remodeling a hotel at Hampton Beach, and they got the itch to do the same. They bought the old Pelham Hotel. It needed lots of work before it would start making any money for them. They worked day and night doing all the renovations, and finally the day arrived. In time they were able to put out a "No Vacancy" sign.

Included with the purchase was a guest house behind the hotel. They had it removed and replaced it with a motel to accommodate winter rentals. Both sets of units were a huge success and after a number of years of working 24/7 they decided to sell at the height of the real estate market. They bought a nice home in Rye, NH right across from the little cottages known as Rye on the Rocks.

After a number of years of enjoying their retirement, Jeanne came down with ovarian cancer. She suffered greatly and died in 1998 at the age of 70. Their daughter, Donna, an accomplished painter, also died of cancer in 2009, at the age of 55. Don also died of cancer in 2011 at the age of 84. Their son Jeff continues to survive them all and is living in Portland, ME. They are greatly missed by all of us.

Within one year, Don's two brothers also passed away due to cancer. Since we can no longer give a hug and say I love you to those that have passed away we should not waste a moment to tell our family, friends and those in need that we care.

(L-R) Claire, me and Jeanne.

My sister Claire

There is no position any worse than being second out of three siblings. It's like being between a rock and a hard place, or a rose between two thorns. Jeanne and I were tall, Claire was short. Jeanne and I were light hearted, Claire was serious.

Upon graduating from high school, Claire married her long standing sweetheart, Norman Dumas. They moved in with us temporarily in our second floor tenement at 78 Broadway. However, due to a personality conflict between my mother and Norman, they soon moved into their own apartment.

Norman was friendly with George Lagasse, who owned a plumbing company with his brothers in Sarasota, FL. George offered him a job as an apprentice to learn the trade. Their first child, Kathy, was still an infant, but that didn't stop them. They packed their bags, kissed us goodbye, and off they went to sunny Sarasota to start a new life. Norman advanced quickly and Claire got a part time job as a secretary in a real estate office. They both took to their new life like a duck takes to water. In no time Norman earned his plumbing license and Claire became Executive Director of the Sarasota Board of Realtors. They had another child, Steve, who completed their family and all four moved into their new home in a very nice neighborhood.

They all came north around Christmas time and stayed with us at the big house. Once their two kids were married off, they were free as birds. I can remember Norman saying that they had done so well in Sarasota that they were planning an early retirement for travel and taking cruises. As fate would have it, on one of their trips north, Norman complained of severe abdominal pain and rested on the couch in the den. They returned to Florida and Claire called to tell us that Norman was in the hospital with stomach cancer and wasn't expected to make it. On July 3, 1983 Claire called to tell us that Norman had passed away. He was 55.

Claire sold the house, bought a condo and married Frank Scarmardi. They were happily married for ten years before Frank died of a heart attack. Claire met Phil Neitzel and they were a pair for several years. Claire had a major heart operation from which she recovered, but shortly after the surgery she showed signs of Alzheimer's. Claire sold her condo and entered an assisted living facility. Phil came to visit her every day from 5:00 to 10:00 PM. Claire's son Steve handled her finances and her daughter Kathy oversaw her health issues, since she is a doctor's assistant.

Claire and I talked on the phone twice a week and she seemed to be enjoying the other residents in the assisted living facility. However, as time passed and her overall health began to fail our telephone conversations became more somber.

Phil called to tell me that Claire was in the hospital suffering from a lung infection and that they didn't expect her to recover. She was given the last rites by her parish priest and peacefully passed away on February 1, 2017 at the age of 87.

Chapter 11

I'll try my hand at anything (Basic 4)

As Cartier Furniture Restoring came to a close, I made a telephone call to MAI Basic Four in Needham, MA, the company I had purchased the computer from for Brentwood Furniture. My conversation with Mr. McGinnis went like this:

"Mr. McGinnis, how would you like to hire a top notch computer salesman?" I asked.

Chuckling, he asked me what company I was working for. "None at the moment, Mr. McGinnis," I replied.

"What's your background?" he asked.

"Well, Mr. McGinnis," I replied, "I have been a Corporate Comptroller for 25 years, during which time I purchased a Basic Four computer for Brentwood Furniture in Haverhill, MA, hired a programmer, and went on line without a single glitch. My Basic Four has been the best thing since sliced bread. If that doesn't make me a top-notch salesman, I don't know what will."

I met with him the next week, followed by a meeting with the Sales Manager and the Branch Manager. After five appointments, they hired me, not because I was qualified for the job, but because of the unique way that I was able to sell myself and the product.

"Welcome aboard, John!" they said with some reservations. "We will be watching your progress very closely. We have never hired someone without selling experience, so don't let us down."

Now that I was on the payroll, my first assignment was a trip to Silicon Valley in California for a two week indoctrination with seven other new hires. The first bridge to cross was the background check, which I failed completely. The instructor asked me what I was doing there. My only answer was that I was hired by Basic Four to sell their product.

The next day I raised my hand to ask where the closest Catholic Church was located so that I could attend Sunday Mass. The instructor's reply was, "I'll check it out and get back to you tomorrow." The next day, the instructor entered the classroom and she immediately asked which one of us was the religious fanatic? I stood up and informed her that I was a man of faith and that she should consider putting a little faith in her life and that next Sunday I would pray for her. I sat down and there was total silence in the room. She told me to see her after class and she would give me the address to the church. She apologized and I accepted. With a smile, I went on my way.

A very surprising conclusion to this ordeal was the fact that I was approached by a Christian and an Atheist after class. They both wanted to attend mass with me to see what the big deal was all about. For the remainder of the two weeks, they both became close companions of mine.

One of the conditions of my employment was to attend night salesmanship classes in Waltham at the Dale Carnegie Institute. Basic Four made all the arrangements, and after being on the road all day, I would arrive in Waltham for the 7:00 PM class. It didn't take long to realize that the whole thing was based on "common sense," so I started to answer questions and responded to written exams based on that principle. I was winning about 80% of the prizes. With my certificate of accomplishment in hand, I gained more confidence in myself, my product, and my ability to sell.

After nine months, 25,000 miles on the VW Jetta, and Laura making fifty calls a day, I was the only one left of the eight who went to California. If you didn't meet quota, you got a pat on the back, marched into the office and were told that you were fired without notice. The Sales Manager would walk you to your car, remove all the selling tools you had and wave goodbye. It was a very stressful job, but I liked the challenge (and the sales commissions were the greatest).

A short time later, I met with Leonard Warden, the owner of a concrete business that made manholes for road construction. After reviewing his needs, I told him that my product was not compatible to his applications, but knew of a person who could meet all his requirements. He responded, "You mean that you wouldn't sell me your computer system?" "That's right, Mr. Warden, you would be unhappy, I would be unhappy, and it would be a lose/lose proposition." He hired me on the spot to buy and develop an automated system to manufacture his products, and also to be his office manager as well. "But, Mr. Walden," I replied, "that's two jobs which

121

require two pays." He agreed and made me a very attractive offer which I couldn't refuse.

My next challenge (1986)

It was in the spring of 1986, at the age of 54, I walked into the office of the Harvey Lumber Co. and sat down in the chair in front of the General Manager, Jack Heath. I told him that I would like to get a job there, but didn't want to interview with Jim, the man who owned the company, as he was my friend. He looked at me with a chuckle and told me that he could use a good road man. "I'll take it," I said. "When do I start, how much will you pay, and what are the benefits?" He sent me upstairs to see Judy, the office manager, who had already been told that I was on my way to see her. After filling out and signing all of the necessary documents, Judy sent me back down to get my schedule from Jack Heath.

"John, you will start on Monday at 7:00 AM sharp," I was told. "You will run shotgun with another road salesman for two weeks, after which you will be temporarily assigned to a Ford Escort until a new truck arrives." He had no sooner said that when Jim walked into the office. Al said, "Jim, meet your new road salesman." "Hi, John, good luck, but don't expect any special favors just because you're my best friend," he said with a big laugh. "I don't expect it, and I don't want it," I replied. I knew ahead of time that if I went to work for Jim, I would give it 110% effort and succeed by my own efforts. I knew very little about the lumber business.

After two weeks as an observer, I was handed the keys to the Escort, and was told to go sell the lumber. I started by chasing Ready-mix trucks to see if they were going to a new foundation for a house. This was followed by visiting city halls to check out building permits. In a short time, I was getting orders, and realized that a 2x4 was just that, a 2x4. So, the difference in suppliers was in personnel and in service. It became my process to personally follow up on delivery schedules to be sure my customers got their orders on time.

As I was getting established in my new profession, the new truck arrived, all shiny and new. "Boy, that's going to be great," I thought. To my surprise, the new truck went to another salesman, and I got his old one. At least I was out of the Escort and in a pickup, complete with racks for small deliveries. It was at this time that I started to pick up my dad almost daily to travel with me. He had a great time and became friendly with many of my customers.

One day, I ran across an addition being built on a house in Bradford. I stopped to ask if I could be of some help to them. The owner of Curran Construction told me that he was in need of some material. I gave him my card and an application to open an account at Harvey Lumber. He gave me a small list and away I went. I returned within the hour with his order on my truck. He was amazed with the service and told me to come back around four o'clock to pick up his application.

I asked Andy, the owner, why did he come aboard so quickly? To my surprise, he said, "If a man will take his father with him on his daily run, he must be a good man, and I have a gut feeling that you will do the job right." As time passed, and dad became a fixture, he was loved by many.

Another time I was parked in the yard and, while I was in the office, Dad had to relieve himself and did so next to the truck. As luck would have it, several of the workers observed the occasion. Two days later, and it being one of the days Dad wasn't with me, the workers decided to decorate my truck with banners and mounted a toilet on the back of the truck. As I returned to my truck, to my amazement, several of the workers were around the truck laughing as I approached. I didn't get any respect that day.

After about four years of being a road salesman, Jim approached me to ask me for a favor. "John, I would like you to take over the Kasher Company in Billerica, MA," he said. "They build around fifty houses a year and I have gone through three salesman and I'm about to lose them. I would like to see if you can save the account. Get their record upstairs and give them a call for a meeting." I gladly met the owner and his two foremen. After formal handshakes and introductions, the meeting took on a casual tone as though we were old friends.

"So, what can I do for you that will keep your supply line with Harvey Lumber up and running?" I asked. "First, fill me in about your operations. For instance, how many different style houses are you building? How many are in process at one time? What area do you cover? And what is your projection for the next twelve months? Before you tell me that it's none of my business, I'll tell you something about myself which you might find interesting. I have been working since I was nine years old and spent eight years at college taking classes at night for my degree. I have a real estate brokers license, and I have a Notary license. I was employed for thirty years as a Corporate Comptroller, and I've been on the road selling lumber for the past five years. I think I can do more for you than the average road salesman, and what I can do for you won't cost you a cent." They seemed to be impressed and agreed to have a meeting so I could present my plan.

The results of our meetings provided me with all the facts to put together an automated system of deliveries. They would start by just a telephone call to me with the start (DOS), house style, now known as model A, B, C, or D, lot number, and location. This was followed by four dated deliveries, and ended with the interior finish. It worked like a charm and Kasher's material problem was solved. The end of this story was quite surprising.

As I was completing ten years at Harvey Lumber, now age 64, I was contemplating retirement and enjoying the good life after working non-stop for 55 years. I met with Fran, the owner of Kasher Corp, to give him a heads up of my retirement. It didn't go well, as he was surprised and disappointed. However, he did make me an offer that was difficult to refuse. His offer was to provide me with a new car and an on-site office trailer. He wanted me to take over the total real estate's sales operations of Kasher Corp. This, I estimated, was to be a six-figure income. I declined his wonderful offer with regret; I just couldn't start in a new direction and continue to work 24/7. I was at the point in my life where my wife and I, and our children, were far more important than money and prestige. For the next three years after that, Laura and I would receive an invitation to attend the Christmas party at the Danversport Yacht Club, courtesy of Kasher Corp, which I considered a wonderful tribute to our relationship.

A life changing event (1989)

Our daughter, Becky, and her husband, Joe, separately attended a religious weekend, something like a retreat. They thought that Laura and I would enjoy the experience. They said that they would co-sponsor us but the husband had to go first. I think that the reason for that rule is that a man can keep a secret better than a woman. That's only my opinion.

Laura really wanted to go, so being a good husband, I said, "Yes dear, I'll go," but I didn't see the need for it because I felt that I was a good Catholic and a good Christian. I attended Mass every Sunday and had always tried to be a good person.

Becky handed me an application a couple of weeks before the weekend. If you haven't figured out what this weekend retreat is, well it's a Cursillo, pronounced cur-see-o. I was told it was a short course in Christianity. With no further explanation, I was led like a sheep to the slaughter on that Thursday night in 1989 at St. Basil's in Methuen, MA. The meeting hall was filled to capacity with approximately 55 applicants. My sponsors, Becky and Joe, shook my hand, gave me a hug, wished me well, and said to relax and enjoy the moment. All the sponsors disappeared and the weekend was about to begin.

I don't want to disappoint you, but the content of the weekend will not be revealed, that is, with just one exception. If you were not sure about the existence of The Holy Spirit, you would be after the weekend ended. Now that being said, we had an Eastern Right Mass on Sunday morning and prior to Mass two altar servers were selected to assist the priest. I was picked to be one of the altar servers. YES, I finally became an altar boy at the age of fifty-seven! I immediately knew who was behind this selection process.

After Mass, the day was rather quiet with a light lunch and preparations for the closing ceremonies and the return home with our sponsors. My wife's opening remark was that I had somewhat of a glow on my face, like I had just won the gold medal at the Olympics. Unexpected changes came over me in a very short time.

I changed like the New England weather

One month after my Cursillo, it was Laura's turn to attend her weekend. On the Friday night of her weekend I was invited to join with other Cursiestas for a gathering known as an Ultreya. It was at St. Joseph's Church and the objective was to reinforce and encourage open dialogue about how the Cursillo had changed our lives as Christians. The closing of the Ultreya consisted of reciting the names of all those attending the Women's Cursillo that weekend, followed by a prayer and a song for its success.

I was very impressed by the presentation and organization of the Ultreya, which was attended by about forty to fifty Cursiestas. After the meeting, I was asked if I would chair the next month's meeting. I turned down that one, but I accepted for the following month. I was provided

129

with the schedule of the order of announcements and events to run the meeting. Why did I do that so soon? This is crazy.

To get direction for this assignment, and for the first time, I attended the 7:00 AM Mass at Sacred Hearts Chapel in Bradford. It is now 2016 and I'm still going to the 7:00 AM Mass. The very first sign of a change was when Father Pische asked for volunteers to become Eucharistic Ministers at the Mass. I marched right up and signed up. Next was for lectors, and again, I marched right up and signed up. Now, hold on a second I said to myself, while you were at Merrimack College didn't you drop a history class because the instructor told you that you were to give a summary of next week's assignment in front of the class and you never went back to that class again? That's right, I told myself. But, that was thirty years ago. Unfortunately, the public speaking phobia was still there. I was as nervous as a witch and sweated profusely every time I lectured. One day, I was lecturing the Friday Mass and I came upon the word "Sadducees" which came out of my mouth as "seduces." There was an element of snickering and laughing, but I rose above it and continued with my reading. After the readings were over, I returned to my pew, sat down and had a little talk with God. Listen, God, I'm trying to serve you down here and I need some help. I'm nervous lecturing, and if you want me to make a fool of myself, so be it, but I don't think it is right. God heard my plea and I was never nervous again. I was finally cured of the fear of public speaking.

I have hosted this Cursillo Reunion group for 25 years.

Chapter 12

He was one of a kind (1986)

Laura's father, Bob, grew up in Middle East Pubneco, Nova Scotia. His father was the cook on a large fishing boat and Bob wanted to follow in his father's footsteps. He loved the sea and enjoyed fishing. There was only one problem; he would get seasick every time he got on board a large fishing boat. For this reason, his dream was short lived. He ventured out looking for greener pastures and landed in Haverhill, MA.

Bob got a job quickly at the Bradford Boxboard along the shores of the Merrimack River. It wasn't long after that an opportunity surfaced with an opening for the sexton at the Sacred Hearts Church where he was attending mass every Sunday. Bob applied and was accepted for the position. It turned out to be a 24/7 position. Bob was involved with the church property, the rectory, the school, and the nun's convent. He was also expected to drive for the nuns and the priest from time to time. He loved every minute of it, including shoveling coal into the huge boiler in the boiler room. The boiler room was his office where he had a list of his daily, weekly, and monthly routines. He also had a clipboard for special projects to do when he had the spare time. He would ring the bells for the Angelus at 6:00 AM, 12 noon and 6:00 PM. He helped the kids cross the street before school started and after school ended. He mowed the lawns and shoveled the snow. I have to stop writing this now and take a nap, it's making me tired just writing it.

There is a memorable moment that I'll never forget about Laura's father. One day, Laura, Alice and Lucy were attending a baby shower. Joe, Alice's husband, and I were visiting Bob, who suggested that we make some donuts. The three of us got up and went right into the kitchen. Joe and I watched as our father-in-law put together the ingredients for his famous homemade donuts. He dropped in the first donut and zip, it disappeared. He dropped in another, and the same thing happened. They dissolved right in front of our eyes. Not wanting to let this moment go by without a comment, I said, "Gee, Pop, they look so light, I bet I could eat a full dozen of them." Bob had made one little mistake; he used baking soda instead of baking powder.

Bob was a wonderful husband, father and grandfather. He was the Easter Bunny. He would leave a dozen eggs at his grown children's back door early every Easter morning, ring the door bell, and quickly drive away.

In his later years he was inflicted with colon cancer and suffered greatly. Toward the end, Laura and I visited him in the hospital. Most of the family was there and he was in severe pain. I immediately went to the nurse's station and requested he receive medication to make him more comfortable. They informed me that the doctor was not available and he would have to authorize increasing the dosage. I asked for the name and number of the backup doctor on call. I called the doctor, told him my father-in-law was in severe pain and how his passing was eminent. The doctor asked to talk to the nurse. The nurse confirmed the situation and the doctor ordered maximum dosage as needed. In a couple of minutes he calmed down and was resting comfortably.

Two days later I was at work and had the urge to call Laura. I told her to call her mother and I would take them to visit Bob. When we arrived at the hospital he was resting without any serious pain and acknowledged our presence. Shortly thereafter, Bob had a strange expression on his face as though a group of friends were coming to take him home. I rushed to his side as Laura and her mother watched in shock. I held him as he took his final breath, and he passed very peacefully. It was another emotional and miraculous moment.

Along came the fifth

For fifteen years Laura was the youngest of the four Amirault children. Well, that ended in 1946 when the stork visited and brought a bouncing baby boy to the Amirault family. They named him Stephen Michael and the Amirault family would never be the same again.

His father called him Stephen and his mother called him Michael. When he was the Master of Ceremonies for the talent show in grammar school, the teacher asked him what she was to call him as the MC and he replied, "Billy."

Stephen was a devil at home and an angel in public. Since mother Alma was in her middle forties, Lucy, who had never married and was the oldest sibling, became his second mother. Stephen, being the recipient of all the attention from his three older sisters, became very spoiled. When he was about six years old I sat him down and told him that he was way too old to be acting like such a brat. He did seem to be better behaved after that.

We eventually became friends and he came to me many times for advice. Stephen Michael was a talented public speaker and pursued a profession as a radio announcer on several local stations. He also worked as a disc jockey at dances and weddings.

As a means of avoiding the Vietnam War draft, I had talked Stephen into joining the navy for a four year tour since the navy wouldn't be fighting in the jungles of Vietnam. He came back a more disciplined and focused person. That period of his life also taught him respect and the importance of family.

He soon married Beverly, his sweetheart. She had been married previously and had a daughter, whom he adopted. They had a very comfortable life together. One fond memory is the Christmas Tea Stephen and Beverly would host every year for the Amirault family. And they, in turn, would always attend our annual Christmas Eve party for friends and family.

Unfortunately, in 2008, Stephen had a heart operation in Boston. Shortly before discharge, Stephen developed three separate infections and passed away unexpectedly at the age of 62. He was the last born of the five Amirault kids and the first to leave us.

The Annual Amirault Christmas Tea.
(L-R) Joe and Alice; Lucy; Bob and Dot and Laura and John.
Front: Beverly and Stephen Michael.

Laura's sister Alice

Alice is 92 years old and is one gutsy gal! After surviving two bouts of cancer and a round of chemotherapy, Alice still goes line dancing at the senior center twice a week. She drives her own car but chooses to walk to the post office and drug store to get exercise. In her earlier years, Alice could be seen riding her red Schwinn bike around Bradford visiting family and friends.

Alice married her true love, Joseph Abate. Ten years into their marriage they still did not have any children. Out of desperation, Alice wrote a letter to one of her aunts, who was a nun, about their problem. Her response was to write a letter to Padre Pio. Padre Pio responded with a suggestion to adopt a newborn. They took his advice and soon arrived home with a bouncing baby girl named Debbie.

This event was followed by Alice naturally giving birth to a son, followed by another son, followed by a daughter, followed by a set of twins. Since they had now exceeded the capacity of their little house, they thanked Padre Pio and bought a larger house to accommodate their family. Alice's husband, Joe, has since passed but Alice still lives in the same big house. She enjoys life every day!

Calamity Joe

The day that Laura's sister Alice married Joseph Abate was the beginning of a life of very strange experiences which

138

surrounded her husband. How do you explain Joe? Well, he was Italian. All his family believed in and fell victim to the Italian Curse. We believe that one day when Joe was very small he was standing too close to someone getting an Italian Curse and some of it fell on poor Joe. A good example of this was when their sons Robbie and Michael were working on their houses, if their father approached, they would immediately come down off their ladders to avoid something bad happening.

Laura's sister Alice with husband Joe.

One day Joe was having his car serviced at the gas station and the car fell off the lift. That's the first time I ever heard of that happening.

Another time when Joe was a real estate appraiser he was backing up to take a picture of a house. He backed so far that he fell backwards over a three foot fence.

And there was the time he got his new car and parked it off the road on an assignment. When he got back into his car to leave, he realized his car was deeply stuck in the mud. The more he tried to get out the deeper the car submerged and the dirtier the car got. He ended up having a tow truck pull it out. It could only happen to Joe.

Another time, on assignment as a house appraiser, he entered a home with two dogs. Joe told the homeowner that dogs don't like him, so the homeowner put the dogs in a room upstairs and closed the door. During his tour he forgot about the dogs, opened the door and two huge Dalmatians came charging toward him. He turned and started yelling to the homeowner to call off the dogs. As he went running out the front door, he could feel the dogs nipping at his backside.

Then there was the time when Joe was sound asleep in bed and he got bitten on his ear by a bat. He immediately rushed to the hospital and got a tetanus shot. Once he returned, he put on his hat, rain coat and boots, and proceeded to search for the bat with a broom. Apparently, the bat had returned to its hiding place. Joe, still in fear of getting bit again, slept on the couch in the living room downstairs. After a long while he fell asleep and dreamt that he was being bit by a bat. He jerked awake and began swatting at what he thought was the bat but it was his eyeglasses which he broke into small pieces.

My next story was when he was doing an appraisal at a repair garage. It was winter and Joe was wearing a brand new long leather coat. As he was backing up to take a picture, he backed into a blowtorch, which set his coat on fire, leaving a big hole on the back side. He quickly removed the coat and told the owner that he was going to sue him for leaving the torch unattended. The man told him to please get out of his garage before he burned the whole place to the ground. A short time later Joe was seen wearing a short leather jacket.

A final story: Joe rushed to the hospital complaining that he was dying due to severe internal bleeding and demanding immediate attention. They rushed him into the emergency room and upon examination determined that he had beets the night before. Yes, ALL true stories!

Their only son for 26 years

Robert was the third born Amirault child, born in 1925. He was always called Bobby and was a gentle soul. He never caused any trouble in or out of the home. At an early age he had a paper route, shoveled snow, mowed lawns, and set up pins at the Haverhill Bowling Alley on Merrimack Street. He did his home chores with a smile, earned all his own money and bought his own things.

Laura's brother Bob with wife Dottie.

Bobby was well liked by everyone in school. He graduated from trade school and immediately went to work in his profession as a printer, which he did for his whole adult life.

He married his lifelong companion, Dot, and together they raised six children. Every child that was born into the family received special treatment from Bobby. He walked them, rocked them, and sang to them. Oh, how he loved and spoiled his little ones.

He had a green thumb too and always had a beautiful garden which produced a huge quantity of fresh produce. Another passion he had was cribbage. He and I played many a game and when I won he would say that I was lucky, and when he won, it was skill.

His wife, Dot, was the recipient of all his accolades. As far as he was concerned, she could do anything and everything to perfection. He always said that nobody could make an apple pie like Dot. However, it was well known that Bobby did all the prep work. He would wash the apples, peel them, slice them, and he laid everything out on the counter for her. Dot would than assemble the pie and bake it.

As Dot's health began to fail, they sold their home and moved into a brand new mobile home in Merrimac, MA. In time, Dot required 24/7 care and entered a nursing home. Bobby was with her every day. After she passed away, his greatest wish was to be with his wife Dotty. He got his wish shortly thereafter. At his funeral, the organist played and sang his favorite tune, Stranger on the Shore.

A very, very sad time in our lives (1978-1986)

Debbie and Peter were high school sweethearts. Where you saw Peter, you also saw Debbie. She was the kindest, most loving young person Peter could ever hope to meet. They were hoping to marry soon and looking forward to their life together.

One day during the summer of 1975, as Peter and Debbie were sitting under the pine tree in the back yard, Peter called to me and asked if I could take a look at the lump on Debbie's neck. I told her that she should see a doctor about it without delay because you never know, it could be a swollen gland, or something more serious.

Peter and Debbie on their way to a Halloween party.

The tests revealed that Debbie had cancer of the lymph node that would need immediate attention. Debbie was accepted by the Wish Foundation, and she and Peter were sent on a ten day trip to the Bahamas, which was their final time together before her last admission at the Boston Hospital.

Our visits were frequent and many. Sometimes on impulse I would drive to Boston and spend a little quality time with her. She would say, "Gee Dad, I'm so glad you're here today," because of this or that. We had some pretty intense

145

conversations about life, death and religion. The last time I visited her she looked like an angel. She smiled at me and said, "I took your advice, Dad, and asked for the priest. I'm no longer afraid, and I'm ready to go. Give my love to everyone, especially Peter, and thank you, dad, for everything. You will never know how much you helped me through all this, I love you." We hugged and kissed and said our good-byes. Our dear Debbie passed away two days later at the age of twenty-five. I don't think that Peter has ever totally recovered from losing his one true love. Lesson learned, you may never know the full effect of the acts of love and kindness you extend to another person, and what will come back to you.

She held the money bag and everything else (1991)

Laura's mother, Alma, was a lovable person. She knew what she wanted and usually got it. She sat in her favorite chair next to the fireplace at 522 South Main St., surrounded by her prayer book, bible, rosary beads, and holy pictures of various saints.

So, picture this if you can. On my first date, Laura introduced me to her family. After all the pleasantries were exchanged, we all knelt down to recite the rosary. My first

146

impression was what kind of a cult was I getting into. I wasn't against praying, I did my share of praying too. But there I was kneeling next to Laura reciting the rosary long before we had our first kiss. Love blossomed between Laura and me. And soon I became close with the rest of her family too.

Alma was a great cook. She always invited a guest for a meal, whether it was a relative, an elderly person, or just someone in need. Laura and I made many trips with a meal for Betty and her husband, John, friends of Alma's. Betty was afflicted with a problem shortly after she and John were married and she spent the rest of her life confined to bed.

In Alma's earlier years she ran a diner on Emerson St. behind the Haverhill National Bank building. It was called the Epicure Diner (meaning Good Food Diner). Alma was assisted by her three daughters, Lucy, Alice and Laura, but Alma was the cook and public relations extraordinaire. She was always able to supplement the family income with one venture or another. She even taught elocution and performed in various shows. Together, Alma and Bob bought a beautiful home in Bradford during the depression and in the mid 1950's bought the second television in the area. They always had a car as long

147

as I knew Laura. The Amiraults were not rich, but lived a life of middle class America.

Alma could keep an army busy. She sent us to the store, to deliver this or that, to go here, to go there. She was always smiling, very charitable, almost to the extreme. And yes, for the four years that I courted Laura, I would be on my knees reciting the rosary. Since I retired four years ago, Laura and I recite the rosary every morning after breakfast after I've returned from the 7:00 AM mass.

Laura's mother, Alma, was the focal point of the Amirault family. To this day, Laura's girlfriends still mention their talks with Mrs. A and how they have such fond memories of the Amirault house. In 1991, Alma passed away at the age of 89. She was surrounded by her three daughters, Lucy, Alice and Laura. Her legacy of charity, love and faith lives on through her children.

The passing of the torch (1994)

As I look back on my father's life, and the impact he had on our family, the first thing that comes to mind was his constant beautiful smile! In fact, I never saw him frown. He never raised his voice, never got mad, never swore, and never said anything bad about anyone, at least not in the presence of his children. My second and equally powerful image of Dad was to see him kneeling at his bedside chair to say his nightly prayers.

Now, contrary to that image, Dad would frequently visit his brother-in-law, Mose, who lived next door to us. On one particular day my father asked if I would like to come along for a quick visit to Uncle Mose's, which I did. We entered the apartment, sat down at the kitchen table, and my Uncle Mose set out a couple of shot glasses, some ice cubes and a bottle of whiskey. Uncle Mose turned to me and asked, "Johnny, how old are you now?" I replied that I was fifteen. He turned to my father for approval, filled two glasses and the third had about a quarter of a shot in it, which he gave to me. We cheered, touched the glasses, and down the hatch it went. I believe that the whole thing was a pre-determined plan, for I hated it, and never tried it again for at least thirty years.

Dad bought his first car in 1949, a '39 Dodge, I was seventeen. Now that was an exciting moment for the whole family, especially Dad and me. As a matter of fact, Laura and I took his 1939 Dodge to New York on our honeymoon.

Fast forward to dad's time with me in the Harvey truck. There were times that I wasn't able to take him. He would get upset for not picking him up and the frustration would linger into the next day.

Dad was in excellent shape into his late nineties. He did his exercises every morning and his mind was as alert as ever. The month before he died we played cribbage together. Shortly after that visit I got a call from Dr. Chaput informing me that dad had a major stroke. I went to him immediately and found him in a shocking state. He was in a wheelchair unable to move and unable to talk. I was devastated. Dr. Chaput took me aside and informed me that due to his amazing physical condition my father could remain in this state for a very long time. Since his quality of life was no longer present, I had a personal conversation with God and prayed that He would grant me three wishes. First, that Dad would not suffer, second that God would take him soon, and third that I be with him when he died.

A week later, Dr. Chaput called to inform me that Dad had entered into a very deep coma without any warning or any specific medical reason. I thanked God for fulfilling my first request that Dad wasn't suffering. A few days passed and I got a call from the nursing home at 4:45 AM, saying I was to come at once as my father's condition had become critical. Laura and I dressed quickly and rushed to his side. Dad was propped up in his bed and his eyes were wide open. Laura was on one side of his bed and I was on the other side. We were both holding his hands and we both kissed him on his forehead. I then bent close to him and said, "Its okay Dad, you can go now," and at that moment he peacefully passed away.

Don't ever tell me that you can't have direct contact with God and that the power of prayer doesn't exist. Knock and the door will be opened. Seek and you will find. What an excellent example of these truths as it applies to my three requests. Everything is possible with God as long as we have the faith to ask God for help.

Chapter 13

It's time to down size (1995)

After thirty-three years of living in our large home at 466 South Main St., all of our five children were married and had gone their merry way. Laura and I realized that although we loved our home, we could no longer justify remaining there since it took all our precious free time just maintaining the property. Together, with pencil and pad in hand, we listed our pros and cons for staying there. We decided that our best option would be to buy a small ranch with a garage and a very small yard to significantly cut down on maintenance. We also discussed the possibility of retiring. After reviewing our options, we looked at each other and agreed, let's do it.

After accumulating forty-three years' worth of possessions, the task at hand seamed daunting until we decided to just get rid of all the clutter. Once that mission was accomplished, we put the house on the market on August 4,

1995 with an ad in the paper stating "Open House by Owner."
We sold it right away and closed on October 11, 1995.

Our new home had to be a small ranch in the Bradford
section of Haverhill. We found it at 25 Upland Ave. It had all
the features we were looking for: vinyl siding, vinyl windows,
a garage, and a small yard. And yes, it was in a nice quiet
neighborhood in Bradford.

The Down Size – 1995 to Present.

We made an offer and it was accepted. I called my
lawyer and we met with the seller's agent to refine the details.
We closed on a cash sale on October 23. We moved into 25
Upland Ave. immediately! Our little house had two

bedrooms, so we made one of them into a den and TV room. That way none of the kids could come back to live with us. There has to be a limit to "unconditional love."

We fell into our new routine quickly. Laura loved to read, knit and watch her TV shows. I, too, was enjoying the good life, which included golf with my friend Roger Goddu. This golf thing only lasted a couple of years. I felt that there was more to life than chasing a little white ball.

A little side venture (1996)

Since I still had my Real Estate Brokerage License from 1979, I approached Morris Piccolo, the owner of a real estate office in Bradford. I asked him if it was possible for me to work part time on weekends to test the waters in that arena. He agreed. It didn't take long for me to realize that it was a very competitive industry and not suitable to my personality. I thanked Morris for the opportunity and decided to try another direction. After some research, and because the field of real estate consulting did not exist at that time, I developed a business plan based on a service fee rather than a commission. The idea was to sell a local house for sale during a weekend "Open House." My contract included a list of requirements that the client had to complete, which I provided, prior to signing.   It was mostly a list of repairs, improvements, decluttering and furniture replacement to showcase the house. It also had to be priced competitively.   Once completed, a non-refundable deposit was required at the time the contract was signed.

Laura and I were a team. We provided an open house on the weekends complete with flowers and props to enhance the property for the potential buyer. By the year 2000 (I was 68 at the time) our new business was an overwhelming success. Out of twelve contracts, we sold eleven houses at the very first open house. One house we sold in ten minutes with a back-up buyer offering $10,000 over asking price. Laura and I did this part time over weekends. Who said that it couldn't be done?   My formula for success: develop an idea, add research and hard work, and apply common sense.

This event changed my life forever (1999)

It was eleven years since Laura and I had taken a vacation. It was about time to get away, see our country, and enjoy each other's company. We laid out our road trip to Florida with many planned stops along the way. We serviced the car, packed our bags, and hit the open road.

Our first stop was to visit Laura's school friend, Edie Owens, who lived in Baltimore, MD. Laura hadn't seen Edie for years. During our visit Edie showed us a nifty yellow Cadillac convertible that was collecting dust in her garage. It had been her husband's car but it hadn't moved since he had passed away several years earlier. Edie wanted to get rid of it so I made her an offer. She accepted.

We were now off to the Grand Old Opry in Nashville, TN. Laura fell in love with Nashville and wanted to stay there for the rest of our vacation. We stuck to the plan and moved on to Florida. We found a motel in Pensacola and a restaurant for a nice dinner. Upon returning to our motel, I had a strange feeling in my lower abdomen. I figured it was indigestion and forgot all about it.

Next, we headed across the Pan Handle, then south to Sarasota for a visit with my sister Claire. After several days at Claire's condo, the abdominal attacks were occurring every fifteen minutes and then every ten minutes. I decided it was time to tell Laura and Claire about my uncomfortable situation.

Laura wanted to go back home at once. I wanted to visit Fort Meyer to go through Edison's museum and to go to the Kennedy Space Center. I still wanted to see Savannah, GA and Edie and Jerry were expecting us to visit them in Cary, NC. By the time we reached Cary I wasn't doing too well. Edie was a nurse for the state's health department. She took one look at me and knew something was critically wrong. She advised us to get in the car and not stop until we got back home. It was now two weeks since my first sign of a problem and my attacks were down to five minutes apart.

We arrived home on Tuesday at about 2:30 PM, called the doctor, and were told to be in his office at 10:00 AM the next morning. We entered his office on time and by 12:00 noon I was in the hospital. After numerous tests for the next two days, we still did not know what my problem was. Dr. Powelson finally told us that I had advanced colon cancer and that he would do everything possible to save me. Dr. Powelson received resistance from the hospital, but succeeded in scheduling an emergency operation the next morning, which was a Saturday.

As Laura and I held hands and looked at each other, we finally were realizing the seriousness of my condition. I asked

God, "If it is your will to take me now, so be it, but if not, please tell me what your plans are for me in the future." At that exact moment a total calm came over me. If Dr. Powelson had waited until Monday to operate, I would not be writing this book. I'm sure the doctor was not surprised to find a tumor the size of an orange. The inflamed tumor had pushed through my colon and was ready to burst. Dr. Powelson removed the tumor along with a part of my colon, my gall bladder and part of my liver. The operation was a total success. Thank you, God, and Dr. Powelson, you were quite a team.

My whole family was in the recovery room when a nurse came in the area and accidentally hit the leg of my bed. My response was, "Did you have a nice trip?" I could hear Paul say, "Dad's back." Following this experience, I endured nine months of chemotherapy, which landed me back in the hospital with major dehydration. It was a blessing that Marie had flown in from Naperville, IL. She stayed with us for two weeks following the operation. I received chemo daily which took four hours. After two weeks I entered the hospital with dehydration. I returned to a modified chemo schedule which was much less severe and lasted for nine months. At the end of chemo, all the nurses gathered around and presented me with a three foot tall white bunny in appreciation for my part in making chemotherapy more acceptable for the other recipients. This was my first sign that God had a plan to use me to help others. This was the first of many future emotional and miraculous moments to come.

An unexpected course of events

In early November, 1995, shortly after moving into 25 Upland Ave., Laura went out on the back porch to discover very slippery steps due to a light frost the night before. Laura came into the house and said, "John, you have to do something about that slippery back deck." I thought about it and figured the ice problem would probably require some sort of a stair mat.

It took me about twenty minutes to put together the very first version of the soon to be Icebreaker Mat, which consisted of two materials that I obtained at Harvey Lumber Co. where I worked. I put together three mats and placed them on the back steps and secured them with a staple gun. Laura tried them out on the next icy day a few days later. She came in the house all excited saying, "John, it works, the ice broke and fell off the mat just as you said it would." Laura's next remark was, "You have to patent this one John, it's so important to the elderly that they are safe with this mat."

I went to work building a 4x8 workbench in our basement to assemble a few more mats. I ordered the materials and handmade over one-hundred samples for family and friends to try out. The result was a welcoming response, as everyone said it really worked and wanted more! One of my pessimistic friends from Newburyport, Jack Ronan, originally told me the mat wouldn't work. However, after he tested it out he asked, "What makes it work, John? This is fantastic!" I couldn't have asked for a better endorsement!

I quickly built relationships with a marketing consultant, an Asian factory representative from Boston, a customs agent in California, and a shipping company from Boston.

With my business plan in place, I purchased a computer and the necessary programs to run the business. Samples were sent to the factory in China via the Boston representative that happened to be the sister of the factory owner. How convenient. It took several months to receive acceptable samples that met my specifications. A friend of mine owned a warehouse in Amesbury, MA. I contacted him regarding floor space. Since I was just starting out in business, I had to control overhead, so my friend offered me two unused 40' trailers at a cost of $500 each. He allowed me to back them up to an unused shipping platform in the rear of the warehouse to be used as a work platform until I had built enough volume to allow me to move the operation inside the warehouse. Fortunately, 25 Upland Ave. had a finished area in the basement which accommodated my office needs perfectly.

My visit to the bank was successful; I was approved for a $100,000 line of credit after posting our house as collateral and walked out with a check for $25,000 to start all the wheels in motion.

My consultant, having obtained a UPC code for her own product, offered to acquire one for the ice breaker mat. She also applied for a website. My order was released for production at the factory. Four cartons which held twenty-four mats per carton were to be air shipped to me immediately, which was costly but necessary. While waiting for the samples to arrive, I hit the computer for the list of all the catalogue houses located in the snow belt of the United States.

After studying the list, I selected the top twenty-four catalogs as a start and sent them each one mat with a cover sheet. A picture is worth a thousand words, and it worked. We received orders and inquiries almost immediately. Our son Jack had recently retired from Lucent (AT&T) with a nice package after twenty-seven years. He agreed to come on board with the title of VP. In doing so, I didn't have to pay him a regular salary weekly, but rather a bonus from time to time.

As JLC Enterprise grew in sales and product sizes, we maintained an active website, a product video for trade shows and retail displays, and two salesmen were added to bring in orders from super market chains, hardware stores, and major distributors.

All was not perfect in this world of ours. I'll give you an example. Our sales rep sold to a national bulk discount outlet. Two large orders came with many conditions. Namely, I had to design a display stand complete with a large display sign, design a carton with skids attached for a fork lift, and finally fifty videos in color showing how the icebreaker mat works. With two large orders in hand, we fulfilled all their requirements on schedule. Shipments were made to different distribution centers.

During this period of time, on three occasions we were featured on national TV at QVC in Philadelphia. On one occasion, upon returning home I spotted a sign for one of the outlets so we visited the location, asked for the manager, and we were cordially greeted. We explained to him that we stopped in to see how they were doing with the icebreaker mats. When he took us to the location, we found the display wasn't on display but rather slid under a rack and some mats were lying on the floor, for which the manager apologized. I asked the manager about the video and he replied, "What video?" It was a total disaster. We found this condition at every outlet we visited. To add insult to injury, the outlet company cancelled the second order which was built and ready to ship. Our losses were in the thousands. Our salesman couldn't do anything, the company refused to talk to us and the buyer was not available. Lesson learned – keep away from the big boys, they will bury you.

Another bad experience I will tell you about. I went through three different patent attorneys, spent over $36,000 and never got a patent. I did receive a patent pending in

Europe, and because they were charging me $1,700 a year for the patent pending, they never issued the patent. Enough was enough; I stopped the bleeding by firing them all.

Full steam ahead. One day I got a call from a woman in Montreal, Canada, asking for permission to show our mat to a large distributor in Paris, France. I gave her the exclusive for all of Europe. She packed her bag of tricks, and off across the pond she went. It was a lost cause because most of Europe have no steps or a front porch to begin with. They did have a request however. They wanted to know if the mat people could come up with an item to put in the freezer compartment of a refrigerator. Europe didn't have automatic defrost in their refrigeration systems. I told Silvy, my Canadian rep to France, to submit a color and size of the item, and I'd see what I could do. While talking to her, I already knew what I was going to do. I would simply take an icebreaker mat and change it to their desired color. No sooner did I get off the phone with Silvy, when I took a mat, cut it in half, taped the open end and saw what happened in my refrigerator.

The size and sample color arrived, but before sending it to the factory agent in Boston, I cut a piece of the color sample to check the match. I told the agent to send me six samples ASAP. I received notice from the factory that they would not make six samples unless I placed an order first. I asked what would be the minimum order? Five-thousand units was the reply. This ridiculous demand was outrageous; I had been doing business with them for several years, and without any problems. I questioned the agent about this demand. Her response was that the factory had to protect itself. "From what," I replied, "I'm taking all the risk."

When I placed my order, Jack was beside himself. He said, "Dad, how could you do that, we don't even have an order yet?" I replied, "I know, Jack, but we will. My test showed a 75% to 80% reduction in frost and ice buildup and it will solve Europe's problem." Samples were received and sent to Paris. Within two weeks, Silvy called all excited; she had just received an order for five thousand freezer mats. Two weeks later we received another order for ten-thousand, followed by another for fifteen-thousand.

It was time for a serious talk with Silvy in Canada. The fire was hot to negotiate with Paris. I asked the factory for a unit count to fill a twenty foot container and I was told eighteen-thousand mats. We sharpened our pencil and submitted a quote to Paris based on the container count. The plan contained a couple of requirements, since we lowered the price of the mats. They were to take possession of the product once the container was onboard the ship in China, which saved me the insurance cost. Also, payment would be made within ten days after boarding.

Shortly after Paris accepted the new terms, they made a request to Silvy regarding an insert they were placing in the plastic bag of each mat. This required them to open the carton, remove the mats, open the plastic bag, insert the sheet which contained nine languages, put the mats back in the carton and reseal. I asked Silvy to have them send a couple of sheets to send to the factory. I told the factory to quote a price for the sheet in color rather than black and white. The cost would include the factory inserting the sheet along with the mat into the plastic bag.

The price was perfect, so we both added our markup and sent it along to Paris. They immediately accepted the price and were delighted with the improved color insert. All were happy; we ended up with a mat price greater than our original quote. We shipped many containers to Paris, and we were paid in ten days, rather than thirty days. It only involved our time to type an order to the factory and type an invoice to Paris.

We had been selling an item I invented known as a Clean Duct for cleaning baseboard heating systems, three sizes of Icebreaker Mats in the United States and Canada, the Freezer Mat in Europe, and also to Bio-Chemical Labs in the United States. Looking back on the last twelve years, and now being 80 years old, I would consider this my last venture as a total success, and I was ready to slow down for a change. Conditions had deteriorated with the factory. The last order I placed was so bad that the product was not sellable, but they wanted me to pay for the shipment anyway. I refused, and told them to send someone from the factory, so they had Huayan, the Boston agent, come to my warehouse to examine the mats. Her conclusion was in agreement with mine, the mats were not acceptable. The factory's final demand was to pay the order in full or they would file charges for non-payment. I told the factory that I might be able to salvage about 15% of the $40,000 order, which they accepted. I told the factory that I would send the funds upon receipt of their email stating the order number, product number, quantity and value of the order, and that the settlement amount of $6,000 was acceptable and signed by the owner and a witness. Needless to say, that was my last transaction with the factory in China.

In passing I mentioned to the buyer for Vermont Country Store, who happened to be one of my best customers that I was considering retirement. I asked if she thought that the owners would be interested in buying my company. She said that she would mention it to them and let me know. This was around 10:30 in the morning. At about 5:00 PM she called me back and said that they would be interested. She told me to call them for an appointment.

My first action was to prepare an exit plan. I prepared my presentation of product and performance, with samples of each. When I was ready, I called for the appointment. The day arrived and we were to meet in Manchester Center. This was up in Vermont near the New York border, a distance of about 160 miles, which was their home office. We serviced my 1998 Buick Park Avenue. My mechanic said that he would trust the car for a trip to California and back.

We got as far as Ward Hill, still in Haverhill, and the engine just died, dead as a door nail. The car was in a bad spot and Jack and I pushed it off the road. We opened the hood and checked the water level, which didn't exist. Jack went to an equipment rental company, located a couple of hundred feet away, and got some water. He filled the radiator and the car started. We quickly drove it to a mechanic we knew who checked it out and found nothing to cause the stoppage. He asked us where we were going. We told him about one-hundred and sixty miles from here to Vermont. He didn't recommend we make the trip in this car. I asked him for a couple jugs of water and, with God's help, we took off for Vermont as we had a 12:30 appointment to make. Jack said, "But, Dad, you heard the mechanic" I said, "Yeah, but he's not God, so let's hit the road and make up this lost time." With Jack as my witness, we made it up and back and the car purred like a kitten.

It's amazing what a little faith can do. We made it to the meeting on time, and after introductions and a light lunch, we got down to business. The meeting went much better than expected. They were getting much more than they thought. We all agreed on the price for the company, and they agreed to buy all remaining inventory at the going price.

As the time was getting closer to the takeover, and my lease in Amesbury was expiring, a good friend of mine, Tom who owned and managed a huge operation that reconditioned medical equipment to be sent to third world countries, allowed me to use a portion of his warehouse space to bring in a number of pallet loads of mats that needed repackaging. Alice and I accomplished this over the next few weeks. This was the last load of mats sent to the VCS. The warehouse was cleaned, the equipment was sold, and after twelve years, JLC Enterprises, the last of my adventures as an entrepreneur, was now history, but not the end of my involvement with friends and family. After all, I was only eighty and still had some good years ahead of me.

Just one more side note to end this episode. My business relationship was quite cordial and productive with my consultant and she was paid according to our agreement. However as the business grew, she could see the potential. Her plan became more evident as she played the lead role at trade shows and at QVC.

I talked it over with Jack and we made a lunch date to discuss her present obligation to the company and what her expectations were regarding the future. It all started with a drink before lunch and friendly conversation. That was until I mentioned that she was beginning to show signs of aggressiveness and in a takeover direction. All of which she totally denied. "Well, then, what do you think we should be doing other than paying your consulting fee as agreed?" "Well as a starter, I feel that I deserve an increase in my fee, ten percent of profits at the end of the year as a bonus and, if you ever sell the business, I would want a twenty-five percent share of the profit." Just after that had been said, our meal arrived, so we put the discussion on hold until after lunch.

After our coffee and dessert, I paid the tab, and told her that it is one thing to want and another thing to get. "You will be hearing from me soon as to the results of this meeting." I immediately contacted my lawyer and gave him an update regarding the content of our meeting. I also asked him to get in touch with her lawyer in Newburyport for a meeting with her and her client, our consultant. I met with my lawyer and brought him up to speed on all the issues I wanted resolved, including my UPC code, website and her termination. We met the following week and laid out our demands in detail.

Our consultant's lawyer was blindsided regarding her client illegally obtaining my UPC codes and website. She asked for a brief private meeting with her client. Upon their return they were ready to accept whatever we were to offer. My consultant was to provide me documents, signed, sealed and delivered, that showed the transfer of ownership to JLC Enterprise, Inc., my UPC codes and the website and a signed and dated letter of resignation and separation of any contact and/or representation of my company and products.

Chapter 14

I'm not cheap, just frugal

It all started when I was a young boy delivering the morning newspaper. On rubbish collection day, I would notice things that might be useful that were being discarded. I would return home from delivering papers and mention to my mother those items I had seen. And, of course, my mother would tell me to go right back and get them, which I did.

Fast forward. I'm in my seventies and taking my usual early morning walk. It's rubbish day and next to my neighbors rubbish container is a beautiful top of the line power mower, complete with bag. Noticing a light in the kitchen at my neighbor Leo Ouellette's house, I marched up and hit the bell. Leo opened the door and immediately said that it was much too early for a visit so go home, John. We both laughed and I proceeded to inquire about the lawn mower out front.

"It doesn't work, John, so I bought a new one," he said. He told me that if I wanted it to go ahead and take it. So I did.

My grandson, also named John, is a very skilled mechanic. I called him and asked him to take a look at it. A week later he returned the mower to me looking all shiny and new. He had cleaned it up, given it a tune-up, sharpened the blade, and filled the tank with gas. For the past ten years it has started on the very first pull.

Every time I cut the grass with my new-old lawn mower, I say a prayer for Leo who has since passed away. I don't think I mentioned that in addition to cutting the grass it has a vacuum attachment and is self-propelled so I don't have to push it in my old age. Thank you, Leo, and God bless.

Another friend in need

Have you ever met someone and took an immediate liking to them? That's what happened with Barry and me. I was looking for a new insurance agent and happened to walk into his insurance office in Bradford. Barry and I chatted for about thirty minutes, and when I left he was a friend for life. We both had the same type of personality, which made our conversation effortless.

Sometime later Barry went into the hospital for a heart problem. When I went in to see him he looked great. I asked him when he would be making it to our weekly Friday morning breakfast at Raff's Restaurant. "You will see me next Friday," he replied. The visit the following Tuesday was much different than the prior one. Barry was in pain and burning up with fever. That afternoon he was transferred to Boston Hospital with a severe infection. As of that day in October, 2014, Barry still hasn't made it to Raff's.

With the exception of his times in Boston, I visited Barry most Tuesdays at various local hospitals and nursing homes. One day Barry happened to mention that he had been a cribbage champ at the Haverhill Country Club. My response was that I have been playing cribbage for over seventy years. Barry said, "Bring in a deck of cards and the board and I'll show you how to really play the game!" Barry won the first two games, I won the next eight, followed by a repeat sequence. That is how the cribbage games went for the following six months. We always enjoyed our games regardless of who won.

One day Barry told me that the doctor wanted to take off his left leg above the knee due to several successive infections. Barry had refused, and said that he would never have his leg removed. "Do you want me to tell you what I think Barry," I asked? "Yes, I would like to know what your take is," he responded. "It's pure and simple Barry" I said, "Cut it off and you live, leave it on and you die. You're just sixty-eight and you could have plenty of pain free years ahead of you. Your grandmother died of infections in her legs and you're going the same way if you don't remove it." The next week he informed me that his leg would be coming off.

Barry went into rehab training for his prosthetic leg and worked hard to learn how to walk again. The lesson I learned with Barry is that there is a time to speak and a time to pray and be quiet. I thank God and the Holy Spirit for the guidance that has helped bring this episode to a beautiful ending. The power of God has no limits. Barry returned home after two and a half years.

No such thing as a coincidence

As I stated in an earlier chapter, I make my communion calls every Tuesday afternoon. On this particular Tuesday, coming toward me in the nursing home hall, was the pastor of All Saints Church. We stopped to chat and I asked him who he was visiting today. To my surprise and dismay he informed me that he had just given Pauline Lagasse the Last Rights, and that her passing was imminent.

The pastor told me which room Pauline was in and I immediately went to see her. Her daughter-in-law, holding Pauline's hand, was sitting beside her and shaking her head as though she had already gone. I pressed close to Pauline's face and spoke rather sharply saying, "Now listen Pauline, this is John Cartier and I'm very upset. Years ago you were going to treat me to a free lunch and you reneged. Now, here you are with your one way ticket to be reunited with your husband Ralph and all your friends, and I'm still waiting for my free lunch."

You should have seen the look of shock on her daughter-in-law's face. I could almost hear her thinking, "What kind of a nut is this guy?" To our amazement, Pauline's eyes opened and her lips started moving. In the past, she would have been giving it back to me in spades.

What a precious moment that was for both of us! I bent down and kissed her on the forehead, took her hand and told her to be quiet. "I forgive you" I said, "and you know that it's not good for your heart to get too excited. Have a nice trip and give Ralph and the gang a big hug for me."

At the wake, Mark, Pauline's son, sporting a big smile, gave me a hug. He thanked me for visiting his mother. When his wife had told him about the nut who visited his mother, he knew it was me.

John, he wants to see you

"John, this is Carol Pische, Fr. Marc's sister-in-law," said the voice on the phone. "Fr. Marc would truly like to see you, is it possible for you to come?" she asked.

"Just give me the directions and I'll be there," I replied.

"That would be great, John, and would you also bring Joseph Devany with you?" she asked.

In 1990, Fr. Pische had become the pastor of our church, Sacred Hearts Parish, in Bradford, MA. I had made my Cursillo weekend one year prior, in 1989, and so began our unique friendship. If he said black, I said white.

After serving our parish for thirteen years, Fr. Pische was reassigned to the Immaculate Conception Parish in Newburyport, MA. Our 7:00 mass group had a going away party for him. I was the M.C. for the event.

During my tribute to Fr. Pische, he attempted to get up from his chair several times in an effort to counter my remarks. I told him to sit back down while I was at the podium. "You're the lame-duck pastor," I said, "but I'll give you the courtesy of allowing you to speak when I'm finished with my speech."

John Cartier, Fr. Marc Pische and Joseph Devaney.

I received several more calls from Carol that Fr. Marc wanted to see Joseph and me. On one such visit, the Bishop had arrived. Fr. Marc introduced us to the Bishop, then continued his conversation with us. I interrupted Fr. Marc to inquire if the Bishop had made a Cursillo. When he said yes, I went over to him and we exchanged the customary hug. Sometime later I told Fr. Marc that we were leaving because we did not want to take time away from his visit with the Bishop. Fr. Marc and I had a special friendship but we can't ignore the Bishop!

Two weeks before Fr. Marc died, Joseph and I were visiting him and I said to Fr. Marc that I would love to have a picture of the three of us together. Carol said that it was impossible, he was much too weak. Fr. Marc told Carol to get him his bathrobe. He eased himself out of bed, put on his robe and told her to take the picture. Our final visit occurred just two days before he died on Monday, December 13. He was sixty-eight years old. It was a typical winter day in New England. Upon arrival, we found him comatose. I sat on the arm of the chair next to his bed and proceeded to attack his shoulder saying, "Wake up Marc, we didn't come all this way to watch you sleep."

He opened his eyes slightly and gave us a very small smile. I grabbed his hand, kissed it, told him we loved him, and asked him to put in a good word for us when he got home. Both Joseph and I had the privilege and honor of being pallbearers at his funeral. One month later I received an envelope in the mail which contained ten $100 gift certificates for a local grocery store. They were mailed from Boston with no return address. He didn't fool me, I knew it was from Fr Marc.

A call for help

In early 2011, our daughter Becky received a call from her friend Freda. Freda was advocating for Denyce, a profoundly handicapped woman who resided in a nursing home in Lawrence. She was born with cerebral palsy and could only move her head, left arm and two fingers. Her mother, who had been her care giver, had passed away and Denyce had been living in a nursing home ever since.

Denyce loved to read but was unable to read unassisted because of her condition. She needed a stand to hold a book so she could read on her own. I met Freda at the nursing home and she introduced me to Denyce. Denyce was excited about the prospect of finding a solution to her dilemma after all these years. I had envisioned a podium on wheels with an adjustable stand to accommodate her limited abilities.

On paper, I designed a stand with the required height, length and width and showed it to Denyce for her ideas. After a couple of visits, I was ready to start building. It was built in stages in order to meet her vision requirements and physical comfort. At each stage of construction I brought the stand in to confirm that it would meet her needs. Each time I came she would smile, knowing that her dream would soon be fulfilled. The stand was finished! It had a clear plastic arm to hold the page in place and a pointer with an attached eraser to turn the pages.

John and Denyce with her reading stand.

This was one of my most gratifying projects. I watched Denyce, as she wore a huge smile, demonstrate the use of her new reading stand to everyone who visited. For the first time she was able to read a book all by herself. About a month later, Freda sent me a bound transcript of some of Denyce's writings, which had been published in papers and magazines, along with a summary of her life. Denyce had been an accomplished writer.

My best friend Jim Betournay

A good friend is a priceless gift! This is how it was and still is with Jim. We met in the fourth grade at St. Joseph's Grammar School and we immediately connected. I didn't have a brother and Jim was an only child at the time. Jim's parents owned Harvey Wood Heel Co. on Phoenix Row. They lived in a bungalow on Margin St. and owned two cottages on Country Pond. They even had a car!

Jim and I were totally compatible in all ways accept our familie's economic status. Jim's family was considered very well to do. This was never evident by either Jim or his parents, they lived a very average life. Jim had his chores to do just like me.

Jim's real name was Harvin but his parents called him Junior until high school when Jim decided to change his name. He didn't like being called Harvin or Junior so we hashed around a bunch of names and arrived at Jim, much to his parent's displeasure. Jim has kept his new name for seventy years.

Rita and Jim with me and Laura.

Jim and Rita became a twosome in their early teenage years. When we started high school the twosome became a foursome. All four of us were very happy with the arrangement and we were excited that Jim had a car. That is, until the back seat was removed to accommodate local deliveries of wood heels for his father's company.

The grey four door Dodge remained as a truck but Jim had a way of instantly converting it back to a passenger car when the four of us wanted to take a trip to the mountains or for traveling to our Friday night dance date. We would all jump in wearing our dance clothes and off we would go to the Nutting on the Charles in Newton, the Commodore Ballroom in Lowell, the dance hall at Canobie Lake Park in Salem, or the Casino at Hampton Beach. Our very favorite place was the one and only Crystal Ballroom in North Andover, MA which had a rotating crystal ball. We always ended our evening with a cheeseburger and a Coke at the Cozy Corner in Methuen.

We have such wonderful memories of our dating years during the late 1940's. Our relationship has continued to grow. We consider our families as one to this day.

On the day this book was to go to the printer, Jim was released from the bondage of almost twenty years being afflicted with Alzheimer's disease. He passed away on April 4, 2017 due to complications of norovirus infection. He was

85 years old. This ended our seventy-five years of unbelievable friendship. However his legacy will live on through his wife Rita and their four children who have all inherited his love for life, generosity and compassion for all. Until we meet again, may you rest in peace my dear friend.

Jim and I have been together for seventy-five years.
Such good friends.

CHAPTER 15

Another bump in the road

"Laura, have you noticed a change in my voice lately?" I asked. "It seems strong in the morning, but as the day wears on, it seems to get weaker and weaker." She agreed, so I called for an appointment with Dr. Seymour, a throat specialist, in early January of 2015.

It wasn't a good experience and yet it wasn't a bad one either. After explaining my reason for the visit, Dr. Seymour sprayed my nose and inserted a devise which had a camera on the end. He maneuvered it into my larynx, otherwise known as the voice box, and discovered a single attached polyp. Dr. Seymour removed the polyp in day surgery on February 10, 2015 at Holy Family Hospital in Methuen, MA. There were no complications but the biopsy was found to be squamous cell carcinoma in situ. Dr. Seymour highly recommended that

I be examined on a regular basis by a larynx specialist in Boston.

The exams on April 16 and July 16 were both clear of any lesions. However, the exam on November 5 showed several lesions attached to the edge of the voice box. After a number of tests, a final exam of my larynx revealed that the lesions had joined together to form a single large growth attached to the larynx.

The operation was to take place in Boston at 7:30 AM on November 30, 2015. It got rescheduled to December 15, 2015 due to complications. On the day of my actual surgery, the breathing tube in my throat was improperly placed by the anesthesiologist, which caused a laceration of the inner wall of my throat. The surgeon stopped the procedure to stop the bleeding before continuing the operation. Since there was the possibility of an infection due to the throat laceration, the surgeon kept me overnight in the day surgery unit. There were no beds available elsewhere so I sat up all night with the pain and I was checked every two hours by the nurse. Our son, Peter, waited two hours before being told that I wouldn't be discharged until tomorrow, which meant another trip to Boston. After being home a day, I received a call from the

Boston hospital asking me if I was okay. During the conversation I mentioned that I stayed overnight in the DS (day surgery). The voice on the other end of the phone immediately told me that that was impossible, nobody stays overnight in the DS. I told her that I was in unit #66 and discharged around 11:30 AM by Carol in the DS. Again, the woman said that could not have happened because there is no person by that name assigned to the DS and you would not have been discharged from there. I had enough and hung up.

On December 18, 2015 I received a three page report from the anesthesiologist. It stated that the cause of the laceration was due to an abnormal formation of my throat, and I should be wearing a wrist band to alert future medical personnel of my problem. I spoke with two different doctors who performed procedures on me within the last twelve months which required anesthesia. I had not had any throat complications.

On December 23, 2015, I was notified by mail that the biopsy proved cancerous. This put the radiation oncologist on alert to prepare me for radiation treatments. The first step was to mold a custom mask which covered my head and shoulders, which would be secured to the treatment table to avoid any movement of my upper body during treatment.

The radiation treatments began on February 1, 2016 in Boston until my final treatment on March 18, 2016. We took a total of thirty-three trips to Boston from Haverhill through heavy traffic for an 11:30 AM treatment lasting fifteen minutes. Since the cancer was in my larynx, the radiation was applied to both sides and the front of my neck. Following the radiation treatments were biweekly appointments with the voice therapist and monthly exams of the larynx. For both of these situations I refused to travel to Boston unless absolutely necessary. They agreed to have Dr. Seymour do the monthly exams in Haverhill, and Boston would provide the voice therapy via the computer.

During my exam with Dr. Seymour on August 19 I mentioned that the doctor in Boston had told me to obtain a blood test for my thyroid six months after the radiation treatments. Since I had been very tired and fatigued I asked him about getting the blood test. He agreed, so I had the test right after my exam.

Shortly after, a call came in from Dr. Wilson, my primary care doctor, who told me my thyroid count was 16, way above the average range of 0.5-5.0. I was instructed to pick up a prescription at my pharmacy. According to the doctor, my thyroid was not producing enough hormones, which was probably caused by the radiation treatments. Dr. Wilson ordered 25 MG of Levothyroxine to be taken one per day, one hour before breakfast. I found out from the intern that I probably would be on medication for the rest of my life. I have been on this med for two and a half weeks without any change in my symptoms. I am experiencing mental confusion along with weakness and fatigue.

Our daughter Becky is an R.N. She told me that in three to four weeks I might see a change in all these symptoms. I certainly hope so, since my daily activity has been limited due to the radiation.

Looking back, I was not properly prepared for my situation. Before the surgery, the surgeon gave me a 90% chance of being completely cancer free after the surgery. If I was to start over, I would sit down with the oncologist and get a complete definition of the need for and the effects of the radiation treatments. In hindsight, I would have refused the treatment altogether. Now that I know what radiation does to your body, I would have preferred to live with the questionable 10% relapse. A radiation recipient, who is a friend of mine, had the same treatment twenty-five years ago. He told me that he still feels the affects. Not planning on that for me! In fifteen years I'll be 100 and beating the odds!

Chapter 16

Our greatest accomplishment

As I look back on my life's journey, our greatest accomplishment has been our family. I am very fortunate to have my wife of sixty-five years, our five children and their spouses, our fourteen grandchildren and our fourteen great grandchildren. My family has a bond that has grown deeper and stronger over the years. Each family member has unconditionally supported one another in their time of need.

This bond also extends to our close friends, Jim and Rita Betournay and their four children. In times of crisis, they are always there to help. They have, and still do, provide comfort to our family in so many ways.

John "Jack," our first born, set the pace for his other four siblings. Jack, like the rest of our children, has a deep compassion for the family's well-being. He retired after twenty-eight years at Lucent Technology as a liaison between production and engineering. Jack had developed a skill that allowed him to adjust a product to the highest level of performance prior to releasing it to the market. That skill was useful in his involvement to help market the products we sold at JLC Enterprises. Jack currently works in maintenance at Exeter Hospital. At sixty-two, he is still going strong. He and his wife of twenty-five years, Carol, have three children and three grandchildren. Jack has two children and three grandchildren.

Becky, our second child, is the Good Samaritan. She has always been determined, passionate and 100% engaged in all she does. She is a registered nurse and is devoted to her family and her church. Joe, her husband, is a top notch electrician, earning him the title of "Mr. Fixit" for the whole family. They live in Haverhill in a large farm house built in the 1700's. Becky and Joe gladly host most of our family gatherings. They have six children and five grandchildren.

Marie, our third, was born with bright red hair. We took her home from the hospital anyway! She was an excellent student and an accomplished saxophone player. She worked in corporate America for several years before relocating to Austin, Texas to work for Dell Computer. The family left

Austin and moved to Naperville, IL when her husband, Joe, received a promotion. She soon became a real estate broker and is currently the owner of a successful staging business. She is also the trustee of our family trust. Joe is in consulting and travels around the world on business. In addition, he is an automobile historian and writer and enjoys restoring old cars. Marie and Joe have two children.

Paul, our fouth, was known by his siblings as "Pauley Perfect." His motto in his early years was a place for everything and everything in its place. Paul was never a problem for us. He married Kathryn, who is strong in the creative and healing arts, and she successfully home schooled all three of their children. Paul found his niche early on and became a talented carpenter. He currently runs his own company, Cartier Construction Co., with their son David. Paul and Kathryn have three children and five grandchildren.

Peter, our fifth and last, still says, "When you reach perfection, why go any further?" He has always had a pleasant personality and is ready to take on any situation. Peter graduated from Whittier Trade School as an upholsterer. He worked in his trade at a number of local shops and settled in at Columbia ASC, Inc. in Lawrence, MA. He heads the upholstery department, along with a joint venture with the owner, providing special technical services to a large corporation. Peter and Jack both stand 6' 4" tall and Peter has a son hitting 7' tall. Our family is not short on height! Peter has one child.

The Amirault and Cartier Annual Reunion.

Laura and I were in our late twenties when we had five children. We truly grew up right along with our kids. Fresh air and exercise were always important to us in maintaining a healthy life for our children. We did ice skating on Plugs Pond, sliding at Winnekenni Castle, snow skiing at the Bradford Ski Tow, water skiing at Country Pond, swimming and nature walks on numerous camping trips, and also baseball and touch football at the Hunking School playground right next door. As the kids moved into their teens, we had loads of pool parties in our back yard. The kids couldn't say that they were deprived. Laura watched with delight all of the activities the family enjoyed during their development years and beyond.

A moment for reflection on our fourteen grandchildren and fourteen great grandchildren. It is such a delight to watch our grandchildren evolve in front of our very eyes. What a thrill to watch them graduate with honors, seek their professions, start their businesses and start their own families. I enjoy watching them play and laugh as their parents watch and discuss current events with their siblings. I use our many family gatherings, such as Thanksgiving dinner, to play trivia games or quiz the family about our country and the world. It keeps us young, it keeps us informed, it keeps four generations communicating with each other.

My greatest relationship is with my wife of sixty-five years, Laura. She is my silent supporter. We rarely argue. We do have discussions which we handle with love and compassion. We would sit and discuss my many ventures and she would give me her pros and cons. She encouraged me to go for most of them and actually participated in many of them. With that kind of support, I never gave failure a thought. She is a wonderful wife, friend, mother, and peacemaker. We are a match made in heaven. I am so lucky and blessed to have Laura in my life.

We have had a wonderful life surrounded by family and close friends. This book has surfaced many memories of the past, an awareness of the present, and an excitement for the future observing our children, grandchildren and great grandchildren fulfilling their dreams and goals in life.

I have one more wish, that Laura and I and our family will be present on October 13, 2027 to celebrate our 75th wedding anniversary. It is possible, with God's help, unless He has other plans for us.

My Closing Thoughts

As I review my life as a child, teenager, adult, husband, father, provider, and patriarch of our ever growing family, I am aware of the awesome life I have had and am still having due to God's influence on my total existence.

I have been blessed with Laura, my wonderful wife, our five great children, the gift of faith, and the extraordinary gift of "inner peace." These things have all contributed to my success and fulfillment in life. Success not measured in dollars and cents but in a loving family and circle of friends.

The world has changed. It is filled with drugs, violence, murders, and corruption on all levels of society. Our present generation is leaving their faith and becoming depressed and suicidal. Our family has not been spared from this environment, and has felt the impact in many ways.

Only because of God in our lives and a prayer in our hearts are we able to rise above these forces and live a healthy, happy and fulfilling life as a family. My departing wish is that everyone who reads this book comes away with one simple motivation for a happier life.

God bless --- *John L. Cartier*

Acknowledgements

My wife, Laura, was my number one editor who checked all my typing for spelling errors. She is patient, supportive, and always there when I need her. The saying is true: behind every great man is a great woman.

Our daughter, Becky, was often at our back door with groceries, meals, or just a quick game of cribbage and some of my homemade popcorn. She was my number two editor and my composition expert. She also provided me with my weekly energy drinks which definitely helped to keep me going.

Our daughter Marie and her daughter Emily were my third editing team. Their job was to organize the items, pages and chapters in an orderly fashion. They also developed the book index which was a priceless guide to keeping us all on track.

Our son Peter and his girlfriend Justine kept us supplied with homemade meals. Justine also made her very own energy balls. They sustained me and offset the terrible effects of the radiation treatments.

Our sons Jack and Paul were always available to provide the necessary physical tasks that needed to be done during my long cancer recovery.

Chris Obert, our publisher, was fantastic from start to finish; he addressed all of our concerns, kept us on a straight path and assisted at every turn of events. Chris contributed much to the design of the cover and layout of the book. Thank you for all of your help and support.

The remarkable thing about my great team is that it was unsolicited. When I told my family about my intention to write a book about my life, they were delighted and immediately offered their skills to move the project forward.

Our wonderful next door neighbor, Bryan Earle, volunteered to cut our grass, rake and bag our leaves and shovel snow from our driveway and walkways.

The Holy Spirit was the director, I typed the words, but my family provided the book. Thank you ALL for your part in this exciting venture. I couldn't have done it without you!

John Leonard Cartier

JOHN LEONARD CARTIER started working at the age of nine as a paper boy. He joined the Navy at age nineteen, married his high school sweetheart at the age of twenty and was the father of five by age twenty-nine. Now, at the age of eighty-five, John still hasn't stopped! When John was stricken with throat cancer in early 2016 at the age of eighty-four, he decided to spend his recovery time writing about his life's journey and the people and events that touched and changed him. John lives in Haverhill MA, a suburb northeast of Boston, with his wife of sixty-five years, Laura, surrounded by his children, his fourteen grandchildren, his fourteen great grandchildren and his many friends.